Tom's Midnight Garden

Adapted for the stage by
David Wood

from the book by
Philippa Pearce

Samuel French — London
New York - Toronto - Hollywood

Please see page iv for further copyright information

TOM'S MIDNIGHT GARDEN

First performed at the Pleasance Theatre, London, on 30th September, 2000. The production subsequently toured the UK and played at the New Victory Theatre, New York, USA. The play was presented by Unicorn Theatre, with the following cast:

Tom	Dale Superville
Aunt Gwen/Susan	Janet Jefferies
Uncle Alan/Abel	Iain Stuart Robertson
Hatty	Debra Penny
Mrs Bartholomew/Aunt Grace	Veda Warwick
Hubert/Barty	Darren Batten
James/Cathedral Guide/Angel	Ian Harris
Edgar/Peter	Sarah Baxter

Director **Tony Graham**
Music by **Stephen McNeff**
Designer **Russell Craig**
Lighting Designer **Jeanine Davies**
Associate Director **Emily Gray**

CHARACTERS
(in order of appearance)

Mrs Bartholomew, in her 70s, 1950s
Tom, about 10, 1950s
Uncle Alan, 1950s
Aunt Gwen, 1950s
Peter, Tom's brother, about 8, 1950s
Susan, the maid, 1880s/1890s
Hatty, about 9 to 19, 1880s/1890s
Aunt Grace, 1880s/1890s
Abel, the gardener, 1880s/1890s
James, about 12 to 22, 1880s/1890s
Edgar, about 11 to 21, 1880s/1890s
Hubert, about 14 to 24, 1880s/1890s
Small Hatty, about 6, 1880s
Barty, about 21, 1890s
Ely Cathedral Tower Guide, 1890s
The Angel, in Tom's nightmare

Skaters, Sightseers, Voices of the House

NB: Hatty has to grow older as the play develops. For much of the story she is about 9, but by the end she is about 19. Furthermore, in one scene she needs to be only 6. The same actress should be able to play her at all ages, but it may be effective for a young child to take part in the one scene where she is 6.

Most of the play takes place in a Victorian house and garden in East Anglia. The action moves between the 1880s/1890s and the 1950s.

SUGGESTED DOUBLING
for cast of 8 (5m, 3f)

Tom
Aunt Gwen/Susan
Uncle Alan/Abel
Hatty
Mrs Bartholomew/Aunt Grace
Hubert Melbourne/Barty
James Melbourne/Ely Cathedral Tower Guide/Angel (in
    nightmare)
Edgar Melbourne/Peter

Skaters, Sightseers and other roles to be played by the
ensemble

ACKNOWLEDGEMENTS

My thanks to Tony Graham and Chris Moxon of Unicorn Theatre for commissioning this play and for giving it such a splendid first production.

Philippa Pearce, who wrote the classic novel upon which the play is based, co-operated generously and accommodatingly during each stage of the writing. I would like to thank her for entrusting to me the adaptation of her brilliant book, and for her enthusiastic comments and helpful suggestions. Our collaboration was a real pleasure.

David Wood

Music

Stephen McNeff's music, written for the original Unicorn Theatre production, is available on hire from Samuel French Ltd.

Its use is not mandatory, but an additional performing fee (plus a nominal hire fee for the music) is payable whenever it is used.

The novel, *Tom's Midnight Garden*, was originally published by Oxford University Press/Puffin Books.

INTRODUCTION

At the heart of *Tom's Midnight Garden* is a simple, warm story of two lonely children longing for friendship and finding each other. But Tom is living in the 1950s and Hatty is living in the 1880s and 1890s. For Tom the friendship lasts a few weeks; for Hatty it lasts about ten years. Their story may be simple, but it is set within a complex structure of "time fantasy". Tom, at midnight each night, is able to go back in time to meet Hatty at various stages of her young life, but not always in conventional time sequence. His visits seem quite long in Hatty's time, but when he returns to his own time each night, Tom finds he has only been away a few minutes.

The story combines beautifully the reality of Tom's two lives. Is it a ghost story? Is it exploring the supernatural? Is it about the power of the human spirit? Does it suggest that an old house can retain memories of its past? Is it about time? Is it about freedom? It is about all these things. And what makes the book a classic is that it is also believable. The reader is drawn into the mystery and accepts the fantasy as plausible and real.

To adapt the book for the stage is a challenge because the two periods (the 1950s and the 1880s/1890s) are both as real as one another. Visually it would be wrong to realistically recreate one period in more detail than the other; and the complexity of changing scene speedily, say from a 1950s backyard to the equivalent 1880s/1890s garden, or from the sparse, utilitarian 1950s hallway to the cluttered, carpeted opulence of the 1880s/1890s hallway would be testing, to say the least. It might be possible using the sophisticated techniques of projected slides or stage revolves, but even these would be far too cumbersome for the basically simple, human story being told.

I believe the solution is to be found in simplicity. Both periods must be recreated non-naturalistically in terms of scenery, yet naturalistically in terms of costume. A basic, non-specific set is required, featuring different levels to help suggest the bedroom, the cupboard, the treehouse, the greenhouse, the "Steps of St Paul's" tree, the sundial wall, the bridge and Ely Cathedral Tower. Dominating the set should perhaps be the two constant factors in both periods—the grandfather clock and the doorway leading to the backyard/ garden; perhaps only the doorframe is necessary. Some scenes will take place on the main stage area, using basic props and, when necessary, furniture. Similarly, the horse and gig could be imaginatively created. It should be possible for the actors to move all the way round the set in vision, to facilitate journeys and chases in the garden. Imaginative use of lighting could suggest the changing seasons and locations, going from interior to exterior and back and forth in time.

The story should develop smoothly, without any necessity for complex scene changes. This will involve narration, a shared storytelling convention, whereby the acting company tell the story as well as act it out; some of the ensemble will play more than one role. Part of this storytelling technique will involve Tom writing (and reading aloud) his letters to his brother Peter, at home with measles. In this way, some of the episodes from the book, especially those set in the 1950s, need not be fully-realized "scenes", rather snatches of dialogue or voices from the shadows. It also means that descriptions of the settings will be verbal rather than realistically visual.

Music and sound effects will be important to give atmosphere, tension and emotional highlighting, rather like underscoring in a film.

Several animals feature in the story, such as the Melbournes' pet terrier, the geese and the wren. When I began work on this adaptation I believed that these could all be created using inventive puppetry. Productions may profitably explore this possibility. But I now consider that the suggested minimalist style of the production favours *imagining* all the animals, using sound effects to suggest their presence. If the director feels this won't work for Pincher, the terrier, perhaps an actor could play him, or a puppet on a leash could be manipulated by the Melbourne boys—but this may feel out of key.

Mime may well be used to help illustrate activities like skating, and also the magical ability Tom discovers in himself to pass through closed doors.

Because they are from different times, Tom and Hatty can never touch; and Tom, when in Hatty's time, cannot touch or pick up objects.

Finally, I confess to an anachronism. Three times I give Tom and Peter the word "wow", which Philippa Pearce pointed out was not current in 1950s England. But words like "gosh" and "golly" seem comical and don't communicate enough sense of wonder. "My word!" sounds middle-aged and formal. We have decided to let "wow" stand until we can find an authentic alternative.

David Wood
June 2000

POSTSCRIPT

I wrote this introduction before Tony Graham directed the first splendid production for Unicorn Theatre. It is now worth recording some of the ideas he, the designer Russell Craig, and the company introduced, in the hope that they may be of practical help to prospective producers.

The set was stark and black, with contrasting white, vertical elastic "bungee" ropes forming wing flats, back cloth and walls. These became trees and secret passages when required, through which Tom could magically squeeze or Hatty and the Melbourne brothers chase. A tall, movable box-like structure, again with "bungee" rope walls, acted as the greenhouse, and its roof was used as the bedroom, the sundial wall, the bridge and Ely Cathedral Tower. A movable staircase, a very tall grandfather clock and an imposing doorway (used for both the inside and the outside of the garden door) were all realistic, but painted black. The tree called "The Steps of St Paul's" was created by three of the actors, who then controlled Hatty's fall.

Furthermore, a chair was used as the bed and there was no bedside table. The drawing of curtains and turning on and off the light were mimed. The breakfast table was imagined. For Tom's nightmare, his bedroom was relocated to centre stage. The garden door was also used as Mrs Bartholomew's door in the final scene.

The face of the grandfather clock was never visible in this production (although other productions could choose to show the face). Tom and Hatty's descriptions of the angel, striding on sea and land, holding open a book, were sufficient.

All the animals were mimed, with sound effects helping create the illusion. The lighting by Jeanine Davies was sophisticated, defining areas and using colour to imaginatively create the garden.

Three of the actors also played Stephen McNeff's haunting music, on cello, violin and flute. The cello also created sound effects for the shooting of arrows.

The production did not use a small child to play Hatty aged about six. The actress playing the older Hatty was able to convey her young self partly through her acting skill, partly by sinking to her knees in the scene to look smaller.

The "voices of the house" were spoken live by the actors, visible yet not brightly lit. Occasionally an echo effect enhanced the supernatural atmosphere.

Props were kept to the minimum. The gig was created with two chairs and a sound effect. Costumes were authentic, immediately distinguishing between the two periods.

Scene changes were kept to the minimum and were usually integral to the action and kept the story moving fluently.

Future productions will doubtless find different ways of mounting the play, but the rewarding experience of the original production suggests that simplicity of staging is indeed a vital ingredient of the theatricality required to tell this beguiling story.

David Wood
November 2000

OTHER PLAYS AND MUSICALS BY DAVID WOOD

Aladdin
The BFG (based on the book by Roald Dahl)
Babe, the Sheep-Pig (based on the book by Dick King-Smith)
Babes in the Magic Wood
Cinderella
Dick Whittington and Wondercat
Dinosaurs and all that Rubbish (based on the book by Michael Foreman)
Flibberty and the Penguin
The Gingerbread Man
Hijack Over Hygenia
The Ideal Gnome Expedition
Jack and the Giant
Jack the Lad (co-written with Dave and Tom Arthur)
Larry the Lamb in Toytown (co-written with Sheila Ruskin, adapted from
the stories of S. G. Hulme-Beaman)
Meg and Mog Show (from the books by Helen Nicoll and Jan
Pienkowski)
More Adventures of Noddy (based on the stories by Enid Blyton)
Mother Goose's Golden Christmas
Noddy (based on the stories by Enid Blyton)
Nutcracker Sweet
Old Father Time
The Old Man of Lochnagar (based on the book by HRH The Prince of
Wales)
Old Mother Hubbard
The Owl and the Pussycat went to See... (co-written with Sheila Ruskin)
The Papertown Paperchase
The Pied Piper (co-written with Dave and Toni Arthur)
The Plotters of Cabbage Patch Corner
Robin Hood (co-written with Dave and Toni Arthur)
Rupert and the Green Dragon (based on the Rupert stories and characters
by Mary Tourtel and Alfred Bestall)
Save the Human (based on the story by Tony Husband and David Wood)
The See-Saw Tree
The Selfish Shellfish
Spot's Birthday Party (based on the books by Eric Hill)
There Was An Old Woman...
Tickle (one act)
The Twits (based on the book by Roald Dahl)
The Witches (based on the book by Roald Dahl)

Theatre for Children—Guide to Writing, Adapting, Directing and Acting
(written with Janet Grant, published by Faber and Faber)

ACT I

Scene 1

Mysterious music

Dim Lighting reveals shadowy figures standing still

A tick tock sound echoes as a grandfather clock becomes visible

An old lady (1950s), Mrs Bartholomew, dressed in black, shuffles downstairs towards the clock

She opens the door of the clock with a key, takes out a winding handle, opens the dial front and begins to wind the clock's two slots

The shadowy figures whisper, echoing each other, rising to a loud climax

Voices   And there shall be…
Shall be…
Shall be…
Time…
Time…
Time…
No…
No…
No…
Longer…
Longer…
Longer…
TIME NO LONGER!

Mrs Bartholomew shuffles back up the stairs and disappears

The clock's hands point to five o'clock but it strikes only once

SCENE 2

Immediately the Lighting snaps up to bright normality (1950s)

Tom, accompanied by Uncle Alan, carrying Tom's suitcase, is greeted by Aunt Gwen

Aunt Gwen Tom! Welcome! My, you've grown!

She kisses Tom, who bears it without complaint or enthusiasm

It's lovely to see you. Did you have a good journey? Uncle Alan didn't drive too fast, did he?

Tom, sullenly silent, looks around

Uncle Alan (*somewhat sarcastically*) Yes, Aunt Gwen, thank you, Aunt Gwen, we had a very good journey. Ely Cathedral was looking particularly fine.

Aunt Gwen (*laughingly chiding*) Alan! Take no notice, Tom, dear. (*She takes Tom's suitcase from Uncle Alan*) Uncle Alan's teasing. I'm sure it's all a bit strange for you coming to stay in this big old house. Not that it's all ours, of course, we just live in one of the flats. Old Mrs Bartholomew owns the house. This way, Tom, dear.

Tom is looking at the clock. He tries to open its door

Uncle Alan (*rather sharply*) Don't touch the clock, Tom.

Aunt Gwen (*lowering her voice*) Mrs Bartholomew's rather particular about her grandfather clock.

As Tom turns away, the clock strikes one. Tom looks round at it again

Uncle Alan Can't think why she's so particular about it. Keeps perfect time. (*He checks his wrist-watch*) Five o'clock. But utterly unreliable in its striking. Keeps me awake at night, too.

As if to prove the point, the clock eerily strikes once more. The actors freeze as the Lighting changes

SCENE 3

Aunt Gwen leads Tom into his bedroom

Tom looks around impassively

Aunt Gwen This is your room, Tom, dear. The bathroom's right next door.
It's a bit small, but I've put some flowers in it and there are books to read.
And a cupboard for your clothes. I'm just sorry we've no garden for you
to play in, and no children living in the flats to make friends with.

Tom (*suddenly blurting out*) I'm not a baby!

Aunt Gwen Of course not...

Tom There are bars across the bottom of the window. I'm not a baby!

Aunt Gwen But the bars are nothing to do with you, Tom. They were here
when we came. Maybe the room was once a nursery. Now, make yourself
at home and I'll call you when it's teatime. I've baked one of my special
cakes for you.

Aunt Gwen leaves

Tom sighs. He looks around and picks up a book

Tom (*reading the cover*) "The Ideal Book for Girls". (*He makes a scornful
face and starts to put the book down, but then takes a picture postcard from
his pocket and rests it on the book to write. Writing*) Dear Peter, fine brother
you are, going and getting measles. Now we can't build our tree-house.
This card is a picture...

*Lights up elsewhere on Peter, spotty with measles, wearing pyjamas and
dressing-gown, reading the postcard*

Peter (*reading*) ...of the cathedral tower at Ely. (*He looks at the picture
approvingly*) Uncle Alan wouldn't let me climb it. I may be in—fect—ious
thanks to you. But he bought me this card to send you. No garden here and
bars on my window. Aunt Gwen says it's a mistake.

Tom (*writing*) Love to Mum. Get better soon. Tom.

Aunt Gwen (*calling, off*) Tom! Teatime!

Tom stops writing and leaves

Lighting fades on his area but stays up on Peter's

Peter (*reading*) P.S.: Aunt Gwen bakes a great cake!

Lights fade on Peter as the clock chimes three times

SCENE 4

Lights come up on the clock

Tom looks up at the face, fascinated. The clock tick tocks

Uncle Alan enters

Uncle Alan Tom! There you are. Come back in the flat, please.

No reaction from Tom

Tom! (*He approaches Tom and speaks more gently*) Sorry, old chap, but
you can't go wandering about like this. We promised your mother you'd
stay in the flat as long as you may be infectious. Your Aunt Gwen and I have
had measles, but other people may *not* have had measles.
Tom Quarantine.
Uncle Alan Exactly. Quarantine. I knew you'd understand. Come on. Time
for bed, anyway.

Tom moves away from the clock

There's a good chap.

The Lighting fades up in Tom's room as he enters

He opens his case and starts to change into his pyjamas

As he does so, Peter reappears, reading a letter

Peter (*reading*) Dear Peter, I can't tell you how miserably boring it is here.
The last three days have felt like three years. Three years stuck indoors
doing crossword puzzles and jigsaw puzzles. I can't even answer the front
door.

The doorbell rings

Aunt Gwen (*off*) I'll go, Tom. It's the milkman. We don't want to give the
poor man measles, do we?
Peter (*reading*) The food's good.
Aunt Gwen (*off*) Have another piece of chocolate fudge pudding, Tom. And
another dollop of cream?
Peter (*reading*) So good I feel sick all the time! Hey, Peter, I don't want Mum
reading this. From now on, all my letters, B.A.R—burn after reading!

By now, Tom has put on his pyjamas and climbed into bed

   Aunt Gwen enters

She tucks him in

Aunt Gwen Good-night, Tom, dear. Sleep tight. See you in the morning.

   Aunt Gwent kisses Tom's forehead and exits, turning off the light

Tom Peter, it's the worst hole I've ever been in. I'd do anything to get out
of it. To be somewhere else.
Peter (*reading*) All the rich food keeps me awake at night. And so does Uncle
Alan in the bath next door.

*Sounds of running water and splashing. Tom, in bed, turns on a bedside light
and reads a book half under the bedclothes. The bathroom sounds recede*

   I've even tried reading Aunt Gwen's silly books about sissy schoolgirls
having midnight feasts in the dorm...

   Uncle Alan enters, in his dressing-gown

Uncle Alan Tom! It's half past eleven. Go to sleep.
Tom I can't sleep, Uncle Alan.
Uncle Alan Nonsense. All children sleep. And lights out means lights out.
No reading. (*He turns off the bedside light*) And you stay in bed till
morning.
Tom Can't I get up?
Uncle Alan No!
Tom Not even if I need to, badly?
Uncle Alan Well, of course, you must go to the lavatory if you need to. But
you will go straight back to bed afterwards. Now, sleep!

   Uncle Alan leaves

Tom reluctantly snuggles under the bedclothes

Peter (*reading*) But Peter, it's not all bad news. Something interesting and
out of the ordinary has happened. Last night it was really, really late. All
quiet and still. I lay awake as usual. And suddenly...

The clock starts to strike. One, two, three, four, five...

The Lights fade on Peter. A shaft of moonlight hits Tom in bed

...Six, seven, eight, nine, ten, eleven, twelve, thirteen

Tom sits up

Tom Thirteen. It often strikes the wrong number. But not...

Voices of the house crowd in on his imagination

Voice Thirteen.
Tom It's always a number between one and twelve, never...
Voice Thirteen.
Tom There's no such thing as thirteen o'clock!
Voices   Come on, Tom...
              The clock has struck thirteen...
              What are you going to do about it?
Tom Nothing. Don't be silly!
Voice Thirteen.
Tom After twelve o'clock comes one o'clock.
Voice Thirteen.
Voice Thirteen. *Then* one.
Tom An extra hour?
Voice An extra hour...
Tom But that can't be right.
Voices   Tom, you're missing your chance.
              Take your chance.
              Take it!
              Everyone else is asleep. Even old Mrs Bartholomew sleeps
              and dreams.

Tom makes his decision. He starts to get out of bed. Then conscience interrupts

Voice of Uncle Alan And you stay in bed till morning.

Tom hesitates

Voices   Come on, Tom.
              Thirteen!
              Look at the hands on the clock.
              Hurry!

Tom puts on his slippers and creeps out of his room. He leaves the flat,

wedging one of his slippers in the doorway to stop it closing. He reaches the
clock, but cannot see its face

Tom   I can't see the hands.
Voices   Open the door.
                 Let in the moonlight.
                 Hurry!

Tom goes to the garden door and draws the bolt. Very slowly he opens the
door. Moonlight floods in. Music. Tom turns to look at the clock, but can't
resist looking out of the door. He emerges "outside". Lighting effects as he
speaks

Tom   (*amazed at what he sees*) But they told me...
Voice of Aunt Gwen   I'm just sorry we've no garden for you to play in.
Tom   But there *is* a garden! A great lawn. Crescent-shaped flower-beds
   blooming. A towering fir tree. Yew trees, thick and beetle-browed. A
   greenhouse. A path, twisting down to other depths of the garden way
   beyond.

The sudden bang of a door makes Tom jump and turn back inside

Susan, the 1880s maid, enters and approaches Tom, carrying a coal scuttle

I'm sorry, I ... hey! (*He steps back*)

But Susan doesn't see him, crosses "through" him and exits

Tom suddenly notices

The hall's different. (*He looks around*) A barometer, a fan of peacock
feathers, a picture of a battle, a big dinner gong, an umbrella stand, a stuffed
red fox ... but the clock's still here. (*He approaches it*)

Suddenly Susan enters

Susan   (*calling*) I've lit the fire in the parlour.

Susan disappears   ~~EXITS INTO HALL DOOR~~

Tom looks mystified. Lights come up on Peter

Peter   (*reading*) It was spooky, Peter, really spooky. Was the hall haunted
   by the ghost of a housemaid? Then the fox, the barometer, the umbrella

stand and everything else seemed to fade away to nothingness. Everything except the grandfather clock just disappeared. The hall was back to normal. (*To himself*) Wow! (*He goes back to the letter*)

Tom acts out what Peter reads

I closed the door, tiptoed back to the flat, picked up my slipper and went back to bed. I thought about what I'd seen. I wondered if it had all been a dream.
Tom No. It was real.

Lights fade on Tom, in bed

Peter (*reading*) Don't tell mum. Send her my love. B.A.R... Tom.

Lights fade on Peter. The clock chimes as Tom puts on his dressing-gown and enters the next scene

SCENE 5

Breakfast

Aunt Gwen, Tom and Uncle Alan mime eating

Aunt Gwen More bacon, Tom?
Tom No thanks, Aunt Gwen. (*He pauses*) Uncle Alan.
Uncle Alan (*reading his newspaper*) Yes, Tom.
Tom Do you ever tell lies?
Uncle Alan No, Tom. It's wrong to tell lies.
Tom Always?
Uncle Alan Well, I suppose the odd what people call white lie is sometimes forgivable.
Tom White lie?
Uncle Alan Yes, the sort of lie you might tell in order not to hurt someone or get someone into trouble, that sort of thing.
Tom Or to stop someone knowing about something you don't want them to know about?
Uncle Alan Perhaps, yes.
Tom I see.

The adults look at each other, bemused

Aunt Gwen.

Aunt Gwen Yes, Tom.

Tom Thank you for putting flowers in my room.

Aunt Gwen Tom, dear. I'm glad you like them.

Tom Did you have to buy them?

Aunt Gwen Yes. I was happy to.

Tom It would have been easier for you if you could have got flowers from your own garden, wouldn't it?

Aunt Gwen It would indeed. But, as I told you, we don't have a garden.

Tom No?

Aunt Gwen What do you mean, no?

Tom I mean, what a pity! It would be nice if there was a garden at the back of the house, with a lawn and trees and flowers and even a greenhouse. Wouldn't it? (*He studies Aunt Gwen intently*)

Aunt Gwen It would be nice, too, if we had wings and could fly!

Aunt Gwen and Uncle Alan laugh

Music as Tom thoughtfully gets up and leaves

Checking he is not being followed, Tom slips back to the clock and then the garden door. Nervously he goes to open it. He hesitates

Tom Don't be stupid. It's there! The garden's there!

The music comes to a climax as he throws open the door. Silence. Tom looks out in dismay

(*With amazed disappointment*) Dustbins! A boring back yard.

A sudden voice interrupts

Aunt Gwen (*off*) Tom!

Aunt Gwen enters

Go back. Go back to the flat this instant.

Tom goes

(*Calling after him*) I'm sorry, dear, but this is the morning Mrs Bartholomew winds her clock.

Mrs Bartholomew enters, listening

She's a funny, difficult old woman and very particular and we don't want to... (*She suddenly sees Mrs Bartholomew. She tries to cover her embarrassment*) Oh! Mrs Bartholomew. Good-morning. I'm sorry. It's my nephew. He's staying with us. (*She laughs nervously*)

Mrs Bartholomew looks stonily at her. Aunt Gwen shuts the garden door

So sorry. Good-morning.

Aunt Gwen escapes

Mrs Bartholomew impassively starts to wind the clock. Clock chimes fade up as the Lighting fades down

SCENE 6

Tom's bedroom

Tom is in bed. As the clock chimes reach thirteen, he sits up

Tom Dear Peter, that night the clock struck thirteen *again*!

Music as Tom gets up and again creeps out, leaving one slipper in the door

He passes the clock and opens the garden door. Light floods in

(*Thrilled*) The garden was there, Peter. It *was* real. And it was there the next night. And the next night. And the next. *Every* night.

Tom explores the garden. Lighting effects brighten and colour the scene

And every night different. Different time of day. Different weather. But always there. Always real!

Music builds as a montage of events unfold as Tom explores, revelling in his new-found freedom. He runs around. He looks in the greenhouse. A bird flies out, making him jump. He watches it circle and fly up to a tree. Tom follows and happily climbs the tree. As he nearly reaches the bird, it flies off again

A girl, Hatty, enters, looking behind her to check she is not being followed

She quickly puts a note under a stone, then starts skipping with a rope. Tom watches her from the tree

A woman, Aunt Grace, enters and, displeased, indicates to the girl to go indoors

Hatty sadly obeys and exits, followed by Aunt Grace

Tom climbs down from the tree and retreats as a gardener, Abel, enters with a wheelbarrow

Abel passes, unable to see him, then stops to do some raking or weeding. Tom approaches the stone, looks down and reads the address on the note, peeping out from beneath

Then he is distracted by the maid, Susan, who passes close by him, carrying a package

She cannot see him. He follows Susan towards Abel, who receives the package politely. As Susan and Abel exchange flirtatious pleasantries, Tom, realising he cannot be seen, perches on the wheelbarrow. Suddenly Abel and Susan part

Susan exits

Abel throws the package into the wheelbarrow, lifts the handles and moves off. Tom is carried along too

They reach the greenhouse. Abel pushes the wheelbarrow (and Tom) inside, removes his package and goes out, shutting the greenhouse door. He sits outside, removes a sandwich from the package, crosses himself, saying grace, then starts eating

Tom tries to leave the greenhouse, but finds he cannot open the door. He begins to panic, then—to eerie music and in slow motion—beats his fist on the door. Magically it goes through and slowly but surely Tom finds he can squeeze himself through the "solid" door and escape. Somewhat shaken, Tom heads back towards the garden door

The Lighting fades on Abel. As Tom reaches the garden door, there is a sudden flash of lightning and a loud crack of thunder. A storm breaks. More lightning and thunder, then a cracking, creaking sound. Tom watches as the sound of a tree crashing to the ground echoes eerily, accompanied by a horrified human scream

Tom retreats and heads for his room as the sounds fade and Peter is discovered, reading

Peter (*reading*) The fir tree crashed to the ground, Peter, and I heard a cry, almost a scream. I think it came from a window up above me. But this is the strangest thing. Next night, imagine the shock I got when I went into the garden and saw the fir tree … standing upright again! (*To himself*) Wow! (*Back to the letter*) And, Peter, why is it that every time I come back after spending hours in the garden, the clock hands point to just a few minutes after midnight? B.A.R… Tom. (*To himself*) Double wow!

The clock strikes as the Lighting fades down on Peter

SCENE 7

Tom's bedroom

Tom is in bed with a thermometer in his mouth

Aunt Gwen enters, looking at her watch

She removes the thermometer, shakes it, and looks at it

Aunt Gwen No, Tom, you've no temperature.
Tom Really? I feel a bit shivery.
Aunt Gwen Well, no temperature means no measles. That's a relief for you, isn't it? Home soon.
Tom I wouldn't mind staying longer, Aunt Gwen.
Aunt Gwen Really, Tom? But I thought…
Tom In fact I'd like to.
Aunt Gwen (*amazed*) You would?
Tom Please.
Aunt Gwen Well, you'd be welcome, of course. But…

She sees Tom smile

I'll write to your mother. Night, Tom.
Tom Night, Aunt.

Aunt Gwen exits

Lights fade down on Tom's bedroom and fade up on the sitting-room, where Uncle Alan is reading a book and smoking a pipe

Aunt Gwen enters

Aunt Gwen (*almost whispering*) Tom wants to stay longer.
Uncle Alan What?
Aunt Gwen He likes it here.
Uncle Alan (*loudly*) Could have fooled me. Moping about the flat, staring out of the window at nothing. I thought he couldn't wait to escape.
Aunt Gwen Shhh. (*Not wanting Tom to overhear*) Can't be easy for him. Away from home. Away from Peter.
Uncle Alan Then why does he want to stay longer?
Aunt Gwen Seems very odd.
Uncle Alan Like his questions tonight. Very odd.
Aunt Gwen What questions?
Uncle Alan All about time. Something about could a tree be lying fallen at one time and then be standing up again.
Aunt Gwen What did you say?
Uncle Alan Not unless you put the clock back. Whereupon he said "What clock?" (*He chuckles*)
Aunt Gwen Do you think he's all right, Alan?
Uncle Alan Then he asked whether it would be possible, no, *how* it would be possible, to go through a door.
Aunt Gwen Well, that's silly.
Uncle Alan Exactly.
Aunt Gwen I mean, going through a door, it's something we all do every day. It's easy!
Uncle Alan Not when the door is shut.
Aunt Gwen Oh. Well, that *is* silly.

Uncle Alan nods and puffs on his pipe. They both sit, puzzled, as the clock strikes and the Lights fade

SCENE 8

The garden

Tom enters and heads for the tree

Before he can climb he hears a dog barking, then voices

James (*off*) Come on!
Edgar (*off*) Run!
Hubert (*off*) Chase, Pincher, chase!

The three boys hurtle into the garden, led by Pincher, a terrier

They whoop and Pincher barks. Edgar carries a hazel-switch, whipping an imaginary horse. They stop, look around and...

Edgar Quick!
Hubert This way!

The boys exit

Hatty enters

Tom watches as she stops, trying to work out where her cousins went

Hatty (*calling*) James! Edgar! Hubert! Where are you?

Whoops, shouts and barks as the cousins and Pincher enter US and exit the other side

Hatty reacts and dashes off

I'll catch you! I'll catch you!

Tom has enjoyed watching the game

He chases off after Hatty. They both re-enter US. Then Hatty stops, having lost the cousins

She finds Abel, gardening. Tom hovers, listening

Abel, have you seen my cousins?
Abel They didn't come as far nor this, Miss Hatty. Are they playing catch with you again?
Hatty It's the only game they'll ever play with me.
Abel Why don't you ask them to let you do the running away, for once, and they do the catching?
Hatty It would be no good. I can't run as fast as they can.
Abel They could give you a start.
Hatty If they did, they wouldn't find me easily once I'd hidden. I could hide better than them. I know better secret places, and I can keep quieter than they can. So quiet, that nobody even knows I'm in the garden at all!
Abel (*kindly humouring her*) Can you now?
Hatty I see everybody, and nobody sees me.

A sudden voice—Edgar appears

Edgar Coo-ee!
Hatty (*excited*) Edgar.

Hatty chases after Edgar. They exit

Tom (*shouting after them*) Go on, Hatty! Catch him!

A sudden freeze. A musical sting. Abel reacts. Has he heard Tom? Can he see him? Can he sense his presence? He looks around, but doesn't seem to see Tom

Abel looks perplexed, crosses himself and exits

Hatty dashes back, looking for the cousins

She nearly bumps into Tom, who side-steps to avoid her

The three cousins silently enter, unseen by Hatty. They follow her, as in a game of grandmother's footsteps

(*Whispering*) Hatty, look out.

We see no reaction from Hatty, but she suddenly turns as the cousins pounce

All Four Gotcha!

Laughter

Hatty Caught you!
Edgar We caught *you*!
Hatty Let's play again!
Hubert No, Hatty, that's enough.
James We'll play again tomorrow.
Hatty Please.
Hubert No. We're going to the kitchen garden.
Hatty What for?
Edgar Apples.
Hatty You were told not to pick any apples.
Edgar We won't pick them, silly. We'll shake the tree and make them fall.

The cousins laugh

Hatty Can I come?

Hubert No.
Hatty Please.
James (*kindly but firmly*) Not this time, Hatty.
Edgar Let's run.
Hubert Come on, Pincher!

> *Pincher barks. The cousins start to run off. Hatty goes to follow, but Edgar throws his hazel-switch at her feet. She trips and falls. The cousins stop and turn back, annoyed rather than ashamed. Hatty, holding back tears, half rises. Tom, sympathetic, involuntarily approaches to help, but steps back when he sees James approach*

James (*helping Hatty up*) You juggins, you silly juggins you.
Tom (*almost to himself*) She's not silly. Edgar made her trip!
Hatty (*brushing herself down*) My pinafore's all grassy. What will Aunt say? (*She sobs quietly*)
James (*losing patience*) Why did you fall, then? You should look where you're going! I can't help you. I'm off with the others.

> *As James turns, Pincher growls and edges towards Tom, who is standing behind Hatty*

Hubert (*turning back*) What is it, Pincher?

> *Pincher growls more, in the direction of Tom. The cousins all advance to look. Hatty turns and stands in front of them, facing Tom*

Edgar What's the matter with him?
James Pincher, there's nothing there!

> *The cousins, Pincher and Hatty are all looking directly towards Tom. Pincher growls. Hubert restrains him. Suddenly Tom sticks out his tongue at them, shaking his head rudely. No reaction from the boys, but suddenly Hatty sticks her tongue out at Tom, shaking her head equally rudely. A musical sting as Tom reacts, astounded. Hatty can see him! Edgar notices Hatty's behaviour*

Edgar Why are you sticking out your tongue, Hatty?
Hatty (*resourcefully*) My tongue was hot in my mouth. It wanted to be cool. It wanted fresh air.
Edgar Don't give pert, lying answers.
James Let her be, Edgar. We'll go to the kitchen garden.
Hubert Come, Pincher.

Hubert pulls away the disgruntled Pincher, who whines, then barks as he exits with the cousins

Tom and Hatty remain, looking at each other. Eventually...   *(both) move into shadows*

Tom You can see me.
Hatty Of course.
Tom Your cousins can't.
Hatty I've seen you often—and often—and often——
Tom When?
Hatty When you never knew it. Climbing the yew tree, following Abel. I even saw you when you went right through the greenhouse door.
Tom (*impressed*) You don't hide badly, for a girl.

Hatty looks cross

   Sorry. I'm Tom...

Hatty doesn't reply

   You're Hatty.
Hatty (*acting well*) Princess Hatty, if you please. I'm a princess. You may kiss my hand.
Tom I'd rather not. Thank you. (*A sudden thought*) If you're a Princess, your mother and father must be a King and Queen: where's their kingdom— where are they?
Hatty I'm not allowed to say.
Tom Why not?
Hatty (*play-acting imaginatively*) I am held here a prisoner. I am a Princess in disguise. There is someone here who calls herself my Aunt, but she isn't so: she is wicked and cruel to me. And those aren't my cousins, either, although I have to call them so. Now you know my whole secret. I will allow myself to play with you, if you like.
Tom I don't mind playing, but I'd rather not join in silly girls' games. Like leaving notes under stones.
Hatty Did you find one?
Tom It was a letter to the King of the Fairies!
Hatty Fairies. Fancy.
Tom (*dismissively*) Fairies! Did they write back, these fairies?
Hatty (*not acting now*) No. They never wrote back. I wanted them to. I really wanted them to. I wanted them to be my friends. To be on my side. But they never wrote back... (*She dissolves into tears*)
Tom Oh, look, I'm sorry...

The sound of barking as suddenly the cousins, with Pincher, enter

The cousins eat apples. Tom retreats a little

Hubert There's Hatty. Crying again.
Hatty I'm not.
Edgar You are. You're always crying.
Hatty Give me an apple, please.
Edgar Or you'll tell mother we've been scrumping, I suppose. Tell-tale tit!
James Oh, give her an apple, Edgar. She means no harm.

Edgar takes an apple from his pocket

Edgar Here you are, Hatty. (*He throws it, not to her, but to Hubert*) Catch,
Hubert.

Hubert catches it and throws it back to Edgar

Hubert Hatty-in-the-middle! Edgar!
Edgar Hubert!

They throw the apple back and forth. Hatty, between them, tries to catch it.
Pincher barks

Hubert Edgar!
Edgar Hubert!
Hubert James! (*He throws the apple to James*)

But Hatty has given up

Hatty Oh, keep the silly apple.
James (*having an idea*) I know! Hatty, you can have the apple...

Hatty moves towards him. He hides the apple behind his back. Hatty stops

...if you can guess who's holding it. Close your eyes.

Hatty closes her eyes while the cousins huddle together. Then they separate
and stand in a line, hands behind their backs

Ready!

Hatty opens her eyes. She looks along the line. Tom has an idea. He goes behind the cousins, sees the apple and indicates to Hatty that Edgar is holding it

Hatty (*smiling triumphantly*) Edgar!
Edgar (*disappointed*) Oh! How did you guess, Hatty?

The others laugh

James Well done, Hatty. Hand it over, Edgar.

Edgar does so, somewhat ungraciously

Hatty Thank you.

Hatty starts eating the apple as the cousins exit

Tom, smiling, approaches. Hatty gratefully extends her hand. Their outstretched vertical palms nearly touch. Their friendship is cemented

Music

SCENE 9

Tom and Hatty, as the music builds, turn to the audience

Tom (*radiant*) Each exciting night, Hatty showed me...
Hatty (*radiant*) ...the secrets of the garden!

They run happily round as Hatty points things out, exclaiming enthusiastically

The rhubarb tubs! The gooseberry frame! The sundial! My secret passage through the hedge! The beanstick wigwam!

Tom whoops Red Indian-style

The asparagus ridges! The tree called "The Steps of St Paul's"!
Tom Perfect for a treehouse!
Hatty The potting shed! The greenhouse!

They arrive at the greenhouse

Tom (*exploring*) Flowers! Ferns!

Hatty A sensitive plant!

Tom pretends to touch a leaf-tip

Tom (*in wonder*) Aaaah.
Hatty A castor-oil plant!
Tom Ughhh!
Hatty Cacti!
Tom (*pretending to touch one*) Ouch!
Hatty Goose-feathers!
Tom Eh?
Hatty Goose-feathers! (*She throws up a handful, causing a snowstorm to fall on them both*)

They laugh happily

(*Pointing to a shelf*) Abel's Bible!

They emerge and sit

Tom Is Abel very religious?
Hatty Very.
Tom Of course! He said grace before eating his sandwich.
Hatty (*confidentially*) So sad about Abel. He had a very jealous brother, and they were together in the fields one day, and his brother attacked Abel. With a weapon. Murderously.
Tom Go on.
Hatty Killed him! Well, nearly killed him. Blood everywhere. Smoking on the ground.

Pause

Tom That's not true.
Hatty It is! Ask Susan. (*She whispers*) She's Abel's sweetheart.
Tom I know it's not true because I've read in the Bible about Cain killing Abel.
Hatty (*with passion*) I shan't ever tell you any more secrets, Tom! Not ever…

But she can't help laughing, and Tom joins in

Edgar enters

Edgar What are you up to, Hatty?

Hatty I am not "up to" anything, Cousin Edgar.

Edgar All this talking and nodding and laughing and listening, all by yourself.

Hatty I am not by myself. I am talking to my friend.

Edgar And where is this friend?

Hatty Sitting beside me, of course.

Edgar (*laughing unpleasantly*) Really, Hatty, once it used to be fairies, now it's an imaginary friend! People will think you're queer in the head.

Edgar goes

Tom and Hatty snort, releasing their pent-up laughter

Tom (*imitating Edgar*) People will think you're queer in the head!

Hatty laughs, then checks herself

Hatty It's not funny, Tom. Now Edgar will go and tell the others, and they'll jeer at me.

Tom Then why did you tell him about me?

Hatty (*eyes wide, tongue in cheek*) One must tell the truth, mustn't one?

They laugh, catch each other's eye, then once again hold out their hands, their outstretched palms nearly touching. They are friends

The clock chimes as the Light fades

SCENE 10

Peter is discovered, reading a letter

Peter (*reading*) Dear Peter, I hope you're not so spotty now. My days in the flat are still boring, but at least I have my nights in the garden to look forward to. You remember we made bows and arrows last summer? Now I'm teaching Hatty…

Lights up on Tom and Hatty. She is smoothing a stave of yew with a kitchen knife

Tom Always cut away from yourself, Hatty. It's safer.

Hatty My cousins used to make these. They played at being forest outlaws. Robin Hood, Little John… I always wanted to join in.

Tom Why didn't you?

Hatty They said I was too young. And then, when I was old enough, they said they were too old.
Tom Now put notches in each end.

Hatty does so

Abel appears. He watches

Abel (*concerned*) Where'd you find the knife, Miss Hatty?
Hatty (*happily*) In the kitchen. Don't tell Aunt, please Abel. I'm being careful.

Abel, worried, goes to the greenhouse

Peter (*reading*) Hatty wasn't strong enough to bend the bow and string it. Abel offered to help.

Abel returns with string. He takes the bow and examines it. Tom looks on

Abel You made this, Miss Hatty? By yourself?
Hatty Of course, Abel.
Abel Ay, but who taught you to do it? (*He starts stringing the bow*)
Hatty Someone.
Abel (*looking around, warily*) Well, whoever it was taught you, take care he don't teach you trouble with it...
Hatty Trouble?
Abel (*darkly*) Trouble for yourself, Miss Hatty.

Music as he looks meaningfully at her, then hands her the strung bow. He takes the kitchen knife from her and returns to the greenhouse

Peter (*reading*) I taught her how to fire the arrows up in the air...

Music continues as Hatty excitedly takes aim, advised by Tom. She fires two arrows in different directions. The third arrow heads towards the greenhouse. The noise of shattering glass. Hatty reacts with alarm

Abel rushes out

Tom withdraws a little. Has Abel seen him?

Hatty Abel, I'm sorry...
Abel I can mend it, Miss Hatty.
Hatty Thank you. (*Seriously pleading*) And Aunt needn't know, need she?

Abel No. (*Firmly*) But do you remember what I told you of.
Hatty About being taught trouble?
Abel Ay. (*He returns to the greenhouse*)

*Hatty looks at Tom, but can't resist preparing to fire another arrow. She aims
away from the greenhouse*

Peter One arrow flew high over the hedge. It might have been lost, but...

   *As Hatty fires the arrow and looks at Tom, the Lights fade on Peter, who
   exits*

Tom ⎱
      (*together*) The secret passage!
Hatty ⎰

*Music as they go through the passage (miming, going upstage and round).
They emerge as if on the other side of the hedge. Hatty stops in awed
excitement*

   Tom, look, the river!
Tom It's not a very big river.

The sound of geese swimming

   There are geese, though.
Hatty You should see it farther down.
Tom Have you?
Hatty No. But there are pools where the boys bathe. Then it flows on and
   on, wider and wider to Castleford, and then it flows to Ely...
Tom There's a cathedral there. With a tower you can climb.
Hatty (*in a reverie*) ...and at last it reaches the sea.

The distant sound of geese

   And sometimes, in winter and spring, the river overflows, even here, and
   floods the meadow.
Tom We could swim, Hatty. (*He edges forward*) Or just paddle. Come on.
Hatty (*frightened*) No.
Tom We could find a boat and see where the river goes.
Hatty No, Tom, no! (*She is really scared*)

   In Hatty's imagination, Aunt Grace appears; we see her US in the shadows

Sinister music

Aunt Grace Harriet, you are never to go near the river, do you understand? Only selfish, ungrateful children wet their boots and muddy their clothes or make trouble for everybody by getting drowned.

Aunt Grace fades away

Hatty We must get back to the garden.
Tom But, Hatty, your arrow…
Hatty Quick.

The sound of geese increases. As Hatty and Tom retrace their journey through the secret passage, geese follow them

What's happening?
Tom The geese are following us!

Music and geese squawking sounds increase, developing into chaos as the geese arrive in the garden. Tom and Hatty unsuccessfully try to bat them away

The three cousins with Pincher, Abel and Susan all appear and, banging pans and wielding garden implements, chase the geese, who double back and forth. Pincher barks

Cries of "shoo", "out", "away", "get the dog away", "drive 'em into the orchard first", "shoo, shoo", etc.

In the midst of the hubbub, Aunt Grace appears and gets caught up in the undignified mêlée

Eventually the geese are successfully banished and everyone assembles. Tom watches. Hatty is hiding

Abel Seedlings trampled, lettuces ripped to shreds…
Hubert Goose-messes everywhere.
Aunt Grace How did they get in?
James There's a passage through the hedge, mother.
Abel How they made it, unbeknownst to me, is more than I know, unless the Devil himself taught them.
Edgar They didn't make it. Hatty made it. It's her secret passage.

Silence

Aunt Grace (*harshly*) Harriet!

Hatty emerges from hiding. She goes to her aunt

When I received you into my house, as a duty to my late husband, your uncle, I expected you to be grateful, dutiful and obedient. Instead, you are nothing but an expense and shame to me and to your cousins.

James Mother, please.

Aunt Grace James, you have something to say?

James (*thinking better of it*) No, Mother.

Aunt Grace Harriet Melbourne, you are a charity child, a pauper. Only the claims of blood induced me to take pity on you. Mistaken pity, it seems. You are a liar, a criminal, a monster. You will retire to your room.

Hatty, trying not to cry, stumbles away, as the Lighting changes

Aunt Grace, the cousins and Susan begin to follow her off, but remain in a group, looking offstage, as Tom emerges, upset. Abel is the last to turn away. He is looking towards Tom. Can he see him?

Tom Oh, Hatty, it's so unfair. Doesn't your mother realize? Why doesn't your father take you away from all this?

Mysterious music and a distorted clock chime as the family group disperses, revealing a tiny girl, Small Hatty, dressed in black, weeping. She carries a doll

As the others exit, Small Hatty wanders further towards Tom, unaware of him

He suddenly sees her, not realizing it is Hatty. Tentatively he approaches

Don't cry, little girl.

She hears him, turns towards him a little, but doesn't really look at him, sobbing into her hands

(*Gently*) What are you crying for?

Small Hatty For home. For my mother. For my father.

Tom (*carefully*) Are they…

Small Hatty Dead. (*She nods*) Oh, cousin… (*She wanders away*)

Tom But I'm not… (*He realizes who she is*) Hatty!

Small Hatty stands looking up at the face of the clock, which chimes. Tom approaches

Do you like the clock?
Small Hatty (*pointing to the picture on the face*) I like the angel.
Tom He's a guardian angel. He guards people. He guards you, Hatty.
Small Hatty I like the angel.

Small Hatty exits

Tom carefully opens the pendulum case door, revealing the pendulum, which has writing on

Tom (*reading*) Time no longer.

Voices echo

Voices   Time no longer.
            Time no longer.
            Time no longer.

Tom closes the door and returns to his room, as the Lighting fades

            Time no longer.
            TIME NO LONGER.

                            SCENE 11

Tom's bedroom

An encyclopaedia is open on the bed

Tom, in his dressing-gown, is writing a letter

Tom It's something to do with the clock, Peter. Time dodging back and forth.
    Somehow I'm able to go back in time to when this house had a garden and
    the Melbourne family lived here. But it's all so real, Peter. Hatty's real. She
    can see me. Yet the others can't. It's so strange. (*He leaves the letter and
    refers to the encyclopaedia*) I've looked in Uncle Alan's encyclopaedia
    under "clothing" and "costume" and I reckon Hatty's family must be
    Victorian—long skirts and trousers—and Queen Victoria reigned from
    1837 to 1901—ages ago.

Aunt Gwen enters

Aunt Gwen Not dressed yet, Tom?

Tom Just looking up something for next term at school, Aunt Gwen. History.
Aunt Gwen Oh. Good for you.

Mrs Bartholomew appears and, during the following conversation, winds the clock

Tom Aunt Gwen, could I ask Mrs Bartholomew about the history of the house? About when Mr Bartholomew lived here. When there was a garden…
Aunt Gwen But, Tom, Mr Bartholomew never lived here.
Tom He must have done.
Aunt Gwen No. Mrs Bartholomew was a widow when she came here. Not so many years ago, either.
Tom But what about the clock, the one she's so particular about?
Aunt Gwen Maybe she brought it with her. Now hurry up and get dressed, Tom, it's nearly lunchtime.

Aunt Gwen goes

Tom returns to the letter as Mrs Bartholomew finishes winding the clock and exits

Tom (*writing*) The plot thickens…

The clock chimes as the Lighting fades

Scene 12

Abel appears, pushing his wheelbarrow. He goes into the greenhouse

Hatty is revealed near the sundial on the wall, playing with a toy (such as a wooden cup with a ball attached to it by a string)

Hatty (*singing*) Alive, alive o-oh
Alive, alive o-oh
Singing, "Cockles and Mussels,
Alive, alive oh!"

Tom appears

(*Happy*) Tom! Where have you been? It's been ages.

They exchange their outstretched vertical palms greeting

Tom But I was here last night. Where are the bow and arrows?

Hatty Abel burned them. Said they were trouble.

Tom What were you singing?

Hatty The ballad about Sweet Molly Malone.

> (*singing*) Her ghost wheels her barrow
> Through streets broad and narrow,
> Singing, "Cockles and Mussels,
> Alive, alive oh!"

Tom What's it like—I mean, I wonder what it's like to be dead and a ghost?

Hatty You tell me, Tom.

Tom (*eventually understanding*) Me? I'm not a ghost.

Hatty Don't be silly, Tom. I saw you go right through the greenhouse door when it was shut.

Tom The door's a ghost, Hatty, not me. That's why I could go through it. The door's a ghost, and the garden's a ghost. And so are you, too, you must be.

Hatty I'm not. You are. Why do you think you wear those funny clothes. They can't belong to nowadays.

Tom They're my pyjamas. I sleep in them.

Hatty So why wear them in the daytime? You must be a ghost. And why do you only wear one slipper?

Tom To stop the door shutting me out. Look, I can prove you're a ghost. Hold your hand out.

She does so. Tom brings down his hand through her wrist

See? My hand went right through your wrist.

Hatty It didn't! My wrist went through your hand!

Tom You're dead, Hatty. You're a ghost!

Silence

Hatty (*tearfully*) I'm not dead. Oh, please, Tom, I'm not dead.

Tom (*putting his arm around her, but not able to touch her*) All right, Hatty. I take it back. You're not a ghost. Don't cry, please.

She calms down

Mind you, I'm not a ghost either! (*He sees a bird flying above the wall and landing on it*) Look, Hatty! By the sundial.

Hatty It's a wren. I think she has a nest up there.

Tom I'll climb up and see.

Hatty No, Tom. James once nearly fell from there. Aunt was furious. Said he might have broken his neck.

Tom (*climbing*) I'll be all right. (*With a smile*) Ghosts can't hurt themselves.

Hatty But you're not a ghost!
Tom You think I am!

Tension as he climbs and reaches the top. He gingerly walks along the wall

Yes, there is a nest. I'd better not touch it. (*He turns to go back along the wall, but stops when he sees the view beyond*) Gosh! What a view!
Hatty (*standing, looking up at Tom*) What can you see?
Tom The river winding into the distance. Far, far away.
Hatty (*on tiptoe, imagining*) Far, far away…

Suddenly Abel rushes from the greenhouse, carrying his Bible

Abel No, Miss Hatty, no! (*He grabs Hatty, forcing her to the ground*)
Hatty Abel!
Abel Never, ever climb the sundial wall, Miss Hatty…
Hatty I wasn't going to…
Abel (*frightened*) Swear you won't. On my Bible. Swear.
Hatty I swear.
Abel Say it!
Hatty I swear I won't climb the sundial wall.
Abel Good. Good.

Abel crosses himself, then retreats back to the greenhouse

Tom clambers down to Hatty

Tom What was all that about?
Hatty He was frightened. He thought I was going to climb up and fall.
Tom Why did he think that?
Hatty He saw me looking up at you, I suppose.
Tom But, Hatty, he can't see me. (*He pauses. With a dawning thought*) Can he?

One chime of the clock as the Lighting fades

Scene 13

The Lights come up on Peter

Peter is writing a letter

Peter Dear Tom, I really like getting your letters and reading about Hatty.

My measles have almost gone now and I so wish I could come and stay with you at the flat. Then I could meet Hatty…

Lights up on Tom and Hatty working on the tree-house in the "Steps of St Paul's"

…and help you with the tree-house in the "Steps of St Paul's". Love, Peter.

Lights fade on Peter

Hatty We could have windows.
Tom Why windows?
Hatty It's not a real house without windows. And curtains.
Tom But it's a tree-house.
Hatty It can be a real house too. Our special secret place. No-one else knows about it.
Tom What about Abel?
Hatty He's never seen me climbing up or bringing bits of planking. I've been very careful. (*She edges along a branch*) Tom, is this branch safe? It looks cracked.
Tom I've sat on it. (*Realizing*) But I may be different. Careful, Hatty…

Too late. Hatty falls. Nightmare music and Lighting effects. Perhaps she falls in slow motion, other actors holding her and manipulating her. She lands on the ground and lies motionless

Hatty! (*He clambers down*)

Abel enters and runs to Hatty

Tom watches helplessly as Abel lifts Hatty and cradles her in his arms. He carries her towards the door to the house. Suddenly he turns to Tom. He can definitely see him

Abel Get you gone!

Tom stares back at him

Get you back to Hell, where you came from! I know you. I've seen you always. And heard you and thought best to seem deaf. But I've known you, and known you for what you are!
Tom Is she dead? Say she's alive. Please!
Abel Ay, you've tried to kill her often enough—her that had neither mother nor father nor home here—nothing but her innocence against your devilry

with bows and arrows and knives and high places. Now, I say, get you gone. (*He walks away towards the door. To himself*) May the Lord keep me from all the works of the Devil, that he hurt me not.

Abel enters the door and slams it shut

The sounds of a bolt sliding home echo eerily. Tom beats on the door

Tom Abel, please. Don't shut me out!

Abel's voice echoes in his imagination

Abel (*off*) Get you gone! Get you gone!

Tom tries to push through the door, but fails

Tom I can't get through. (*Turning front, terrified*) I can't get back! I can't get back! (*He slides, defeated, to the ground*) Hatty!

The clock strikes

Voices (*echoing*) Time ... no ... longer!

Black-out

INTERVAL

ACT II

Scene 1

Mysterious music

Dim lighting reveals shadowy figures standing still

Mrs Bartholomew shuffles downstairs to the clock. She doesn't wind it this time, just faces it and stares up at the angel on the face (as Small Hatty did earlier)

The shadowy figures whisper, echoing each other, rising to a loud climax

Voices   And there shall be…
Shall be…
Shall be…
Time…
Time…
No…
No…
Longer…
Longer…
TIME NO LONGER!

The tick-tock of the clock increases in volume, louder and louder, as Mrs Bartholomew and the shadowy figures silently exit, revealing Tom crouching by the back door, where we last saw him

Suddenly the tick-tock sound stops abruptly, "waking" Tom, who looks about, scared. He pushes himself against the door, but cannot pass through. He despairingly gives up

Abel comes out of the door. He passes Tom, who follows him

Tom Abel.

Abel carries on walking

Abel, please, how is Hatty?

Abel doesn't react. Tom cuts in front of him, facing him squarely

Abel, please. I know you can see me.

Abel stops, but won't acknowledge Tom

Abel, she's not dead, is she? She's not dead?

Abel eventually looks at Tom, partly in fear, partly in pity

Abel No. She's alive. (*He looks away again and walks to the greenhouse*)
Tom Oh, Peter, I was so relieved. But did Abel mean Hatty was *just* alive
or even "alive but can't live long"?

Lights fade up on Peter, reading a letter

Peter (*reading*) I had to find out.

Tom acts out what Peter reads

I slipped inside. This time the furniture in the hall didn't dissolve into
nothingness. The barometer, the pictures, the dinner gong, the stuffed red
fox ... they all stayed. The clock was there, of course...

The sound of the clock ticking

...with the angel, striding on sea and land, holding open a book. I listened
to the clock tick-tick-tocking like a human heartbeat.
Tom Please, let it be Hatty's heart!
Peter The house felt strange, but friendly.

The voices of the house fill Tom's imagination

Voices   Come on, Tom...
                  Find Hatty. She's waiting...
                  Climb the stairs...
                  Hurry, Tom, hurry!

Tom starts to climb the stairs. A door slams, making him stop

Below, Susan, the maid, carrying a tray, enters and exits

Tom continues

Peter On the landing I found a door. And another. And another. But which was Hatty's? I started to go through one, when suddenly...

A door slams

> *A young man enters, carrying office ledgers. He passes Tom and calls through a door. We do not yet realize it is James, grown older than when we last saw him*

James Mother?
Aunt Grace (*off*) Who is it?
James James. I'm home from the office.
Tom James?
Aunt Grace You can come in. I'm dressing for dinner.

> *James enters. Tom follows*

The Lights fade a little as Aunt Grace and James take their positions for the next scene. The Lights stay up on Peter

Peter Peter, this James was a man. Last time I saw him, in the garden, he was not much older than me. How could so much Melbourne time pass in so little of *my* time?

SCENE 2

Lights up in Aunt Grace's bedroom. The Lights fade on Peter. During the scene Aunt Grace puts on her earrings and, assisted by James, her necklace

James How is Hatty?
Aunt Grace Hatty will do well enough.
James Is that what the doctor says?
Aunt Grace Yes.
James We must be thankful then.
Aunt Grace Thankful! Thankful! But what was she doing to have the accident? Climbing trees, if you please! Has she no sense of what is fitting to her sex and to her age now? She is old enough to know better!
James Hatty is young for her age. Perhaps it comes from her being by herself so much—playing alone—always in the garden.
Aunt Grace (*accusingly*) Oh, you are always kind to her! And so she is never

to grow up! What is to happen to her if so? I don't know. She's a strange enough girl as it is.

James Of course Hatty will grow up. But what is to become of her *then*?

Aunt Grace She's not to expect anything more from me, surely. I have given her charity enough.

James In that case, Mother, she will have to earn her own living, somehow, although how she is to do that I don't know. Or perhaps she will marry— although, again, she knows no-one and meets no-one outside this house and garden.

Aunt Grace (*meaningfully*) I will not have her ruling in this house when I am gone.

James What do you mean, Mother?

Aunt Grace You and Hubert and Edgar are all grown now, and in your father's business, and independent as far as that goes. Very well, but if any of you thinks later of marrying Harriet, do not expect ever to have a penny from me. Hubert has never cared for the girl, and I believe Edgar dislikes her, but you have pitied her.

James (*after a pause*) I have had no intention of ever marrying Hatty. I don't suppose that I ever shall have. But she is certainly to be pitied.

Aunt Grace She is pitiable, certainly.

James And surely, Mother, now she is growing up, she should see more of the world than this house and the garden can show her. She should meet more people; she should make more acquaintances. She should make friends. When we make up parties of our friends we must encourage her to join them. Boating on the river, and picnics. Cricket matches to watch. Whist drives. Carol singing at Christmas…

Aunt Grace She doesn't want to grow up. She wants only her garden.

James We could make her want more. I'll go to her now, and talk to her and say that, when she is quite well again, she must go in for a more sociable life. I'll say that we all want her to go out, to make friends.

Aunt Grace coldly fails to respond

Can I say that you wish it, Mother?

Tom advances a little to catch Aunt Grace's response

Aunt Grace You will waste your pity and your breath with Harriet.

James Can I at least say that you agree?

Aunt Grace You can say what you like to her. You can do what you like with her. And the less I see of her the better.

James shakes his head and starts to exit

Tom cannot help putting his tongue out at Aunt Grace before leaving. The Lighting fades down on Aunt Grace and picks up on Tom

Tom Peter, she was so horrible. To be shut up with Aunt Gwen all day is bad enough, but at least Aunt Gwen tries to be kind. Think of poor Hatty, shut up all day with *that* monster of an aunt!

Lights up on Peter, reading a letter. Tom makes his way to his/Hatty's bedroom

Peter (*reading*) I followed James to Hatty's room and waited outside while James talked to her. And, Peter, I suddenly realized…
Tom Hatty's in *my* room!

James emerges, closing the door

The Lighting fades on Peter. Mysterious music as Tom presses his body against Hatty's door and begins to magically pass though

SCENE 3

Lights up on Hatty in bed, with a bandage round her head, and a tray on her lap. She is older than when we last saw her, at least she behaves somewhat more maturely. Whereas Tom has, of course, not aged at all. During the scene the Light fades, towards dusk, to the point where Susan enters with a lamp

Hatty (*seeing the early stages of Tom's magical arrival*) Tom! Come through slowly! Please! I want to see how you do it!
Tom (*pushing through all the way*) Hallo, Hatty! It's a knack really. There!
Hatty Oh, I wish I could do that!
Tom How are you?

They exchange their outstretched vertical palms greeting

Hatty Very well. And the doctor says the scar won't show. And cousin James has visited me.
Tom I know. I saw him.
Hatty Did he see you?
Tom Of course not.
Hatty He says I must do other things besides falling out of trees, in the future.
Tom (*sensing the truth*) Things without me?
Hatty (*speaking as a near-adult to a child*) Oh no, Tom. Whenever you want to come, so you shall!

Tom nods, unconvinced

Sit down and talk to me!

Tom sits on the end of the bed

Tom I like your room.
Hatty So do I. I've had it since I was little. It was my nursery. (*She smiles*) The bars are still across the windows.
Tom (*remembering his room*) I know. (*Suddenly noticing*) You have two windows. I only have one. (*Suddenly working it out*) Where's your bathroom?
Hatty (*never having heard the word*) Bathroom?
Tom Where do you have your bath?
Hatty In here, of course.
Tom In here? How?
Hatty There's a tin bath. And Susan carries cans of hot water up from the kitchen. In winter I have my bath by the fire.
Tom You could make a proper bathroom here. Run a partition down the middle of the room, so there'd be a window either side. Then you'd have a bedroom and a bathroom.
Hatty I wouldn't like that. My bedroom would be only half the size!
Tom True. (*He remembers*) And you'd always be able to hear the bath-water next door.
Hatty (*bemused*) I'd never want to hear that.

The Light has faded to dusk level

Tom I don't suppose you ever will. (*Thoughtfully*) Other people may.

There is a knock on the door and Susan enters with an oil lamp

Tom retreats to the window

Susan Finished your bread and milk, Miss Hatty? (*She stands the oil lamp on the bedside table and makes it shine brightly*)
Hatty Yes, thank you, Susan.

Susan draws the curtains, covering Tom

Susan Soon be dark, Miss Hatty. (*She collects Hatty's tray*) Good-night.
Hatty Good-night.

Susan goes

Tom emerges, laughing, from behind the curtains

(*Laughing too*) Just as well she can't see you! (*Excitedly changing the subject*) Tom, guess what's in that cupboard.

Tom My clothes. (*Realizing what he has said*) I mean, I keep my clothes in *my* cupboard.

Hatty (*jumping out of bed and opening the cupboard*) Look! My secret hiding place. Under the floorboards. (*She brings out a bundle and opens it. She picks out some objects: a book, the cup and ball game we saw earlier, then...*) My doll. My mother and father gave her to me. When I came here she was all I had. (*She finds a photograph*) Look, here they are, long ago. Do you remember, Tom, I used to pretend they were...

Tom A King and Queen.

Hatty nods, looking affectionately at the photograph. The grandfather clock chimes six

Hatty Nearly dinner time. (*She packs away her treasures, replacing them in the cupboard*) Not for me, of course. For the others.

Tom Hatty, that clock. What does the picture on it mean?

Hatty The angel?

Tom Yes. And it says "Time no longer".

Hatty Something from the Bible, I think. There's a chapter and a verse number.

Tom I didn't see that. (*Suddenly*) Let's go and look.

Hatty Now?

Tom Yes.

Hatty I'm meant to be in bed!

Tom Please, Hatty, it's important. I want to understand. Please!

Hatty (*after a pause*) All right.

SCENE 4

Music as Hatty puts on her dressing-gown, takes the oil-lamp and leads Tom out of the room, first checking the coast is clear

Tension as they carefully go downstairs and reach the clock. Suddenly the dinner gong sounds. Hatty almost panics. Shielding the oil-lamp, she hides in the shadows of the clock or retreats up a few stairs. Tom joins her

In procession, Aunt Grace, James, Hubert, and Edgar pass the clock on their way to the dining room

*When they have disappeared from view and a door slams, Hatty and Tom
gingerly emerge*

*Hatty carefully opens the pendulum door of the clock and shines the oil lamp
inside. Tom peers in*

Tom (*reading*) Time no longer. (*He finds an extra line*) Rev. X, one dash six.
Hatty (*whispering*) The Book of Revelation, Chapter ten, verses one to six.
Tom What does that say?
Hatty I don't know, Tom. It's in the Bible.
Tom We need a Bible, Hatty. To look it up.
Hatty Not *now*, Tom. I'm meant to be in bed.
Tom (*suddenly remembering*) Abel's Bible! You showed me it, remember?
Hatty Abel's Bible? But it's in the greenhouse!
Tom Come on, then.
Hatty But it's dark outside!
Tom Quick, Hatty, please!
Hatty But what if Aunt Grace finds out?
Tom She won't! She's busy stuffing her fat face!
Hatty Tom!
Tom Sorry, but, Hatty, come on!

*Music as they carefully cross to the garden door, go outside and make their
way to the greenhouse. It is quite dark so Hatty uses the oil-lamp to light the
way. They arrive. Hatty puts down the lamp and climbs up to reach Abel's
Bible. (If necessary they come outside to read it)*

Hatty (*opening the Bible*) It's the last book. One John, Two John, Three
John, Jude… Revelation!
Tom Chapter ten, verses one to six.

Mysterious music under

Hatty (*reading*) "And I saw another mighty angel come down from heaven,
clothed with a cloud: and a rainbow was upon his head, and his face was
as it were the sun, and his feet as pillars of fire: and he had in his hand a little
book open: and he set his right foot upon the sea, and his left foot on the
earth, and cried with a loud voice, as when a lion roareth: and when he had
cried, seven thunders uttered their voices."

A shadowy figure, Abel, unseen by Hatty and Tom, approaches

"And when the seven thunders had uttered their voices, I was about to
write: and I heard a voice from heaven saying unto me…"

Abel Is that you, Miss Hatty?

Hatty and Tom jump and gasp in fright

Hatty (*recovering*) Abel! You made us jump! (*Realizing*) Me, I mean. You made me jump.

Abel Just checking the furnace in the heating-house, Miss Hatty. (*He sees Tom, though Hatty doesn't realize*) May the Lord keep me from all the works of the Devil...

Hatty Abel, I'm sorry. I shouldn't be here, but, please, I wanted to look something up in the Bible.

Abel (*calming*) The Bible?

Hatty Yes, *your* Bible. I'm very sorry if you object.

Tom is smiling at Abel

Abel No... No... For there's Truth in that book, Miss Hatty. Truth and Salvation. (*He looks at Tom*) Them that reads in that book—no, they cannot be altogether damned. If you take my meaning...

Tom nods. Abel touches his forelock

Hatty Thanks, Abel.

Abel leaves

Hatty looks, relieved, at Tom

(*Reading*) "...and I heard a voice from heaven saying unto me:

Tom (*reading*) Seal up those things which the seven thunders uttered, and write them not."

As Tom reads, voices echo in counterpoint, starting softly and rising to a crescendo

"And the angel which I saw stand upon the sea and upon the earth lifted up his hand to heaven, and swore by him that liveth for ever and ever, who created heaven, and the things that therein are, and the earth, and the things that therein are, and the sea, and the things which are therein, that there should be... TIME NO LONGER!"	**Voices** (*together*) Time no longer Time no longer Time no longer TIME NO LONGER

Silence

I don't understand.

Hatty I don't think *anyone* understands the Book of Revelation. (*She closes the Bible*) It's full of strange sayings and angels and beasts and thunder. (*She replaces the Bible on the shelf*)

Tom But what does it mean, time no longer?

Hatty Maybe when the Last Trump sounds ... the end of the world...

Tom The end of time...

Hatty Tell you what...

Tom What?

Hatty It's time... I was back in bed!

They laugh. Music as they return to the door, into the house, and up to Hatty's room. They make sure no-one sees them. Hatty gets into bed. She turns down the oil-lamp

Good-night, Tom.

Tom I'll see you tomorrow.

Hatty (*settling down*) You always say that, and then it's often months and months before you come back again.

Tom I come every night!

Hatty (*sleepily*) Months and months.

Tom (*with a sudden idea*) If I stayed here tonight, Hatty, you'd definitely see me tomorrow.

Hatty Mmmmmm.

Tom Shall I?

No reply. Tom makes his decision. He crouches down on the floor, resting his head on the bed. He goes to sleep. The Lighting fades

SCENE 5

The clock chimes five times

Lights up in the hall

Mrs Bartholomew descends the stairs, carrying a shopping basket and wearing her hat and coat. As she begins to exit she is stopped in her tracks by a voice

Aunt Gwen (*off*) Alan! (*A fearful cry*) Alan!

Aunt Gwen enters, hair in curlers, wearing a dressing-gown. She carries one of Tom's slippers

She looks wildly about, then suddenly sees Mrs Bartholomew, who looks on, eyes wide, at this unseemly behaviour

(*Trying to cover her concern*) Mrs Bartholomew! Good-morning! So sorry, just looking for my husband! (*She hides the slipper*) Going to the shops? (*She realizes she is improperly dressed*) Excuse my attire! Saturday! Later start to the day!

Mrs Bartholomew impassively looks on

Uncle Alan dashes on, wearing a vest and with shaving foam covering half of his face. He carries a razor

Uncle Alan Gwen? What on earth is it? (*He sees Mrs Bartholomew*) Mrs Bartholomew! So sorry! Thought there'd been an accident. (*He laughs lamely*)

Mrs Bartholomew calmly exits

Gwen, for heaven's sake!
Aunt Gwen (*showing him the slipper*) Look, look!
Uncle Alan A slipper.
Aunt Gwen (*rising to a panic*) Tom's slipper. The door was open! This was on the floor.
Uncle Alan Sounds a bit like Cinderella!
Aunt Gwen Alan, it's serious. Tom's gone!
Uncle Alan Hang on, hang on. Are you sure? Have you checked his room…
Aunt Gwen He's not in his bed.
Uncle Alan …thoroughly?
Aunt Gwen Well, no.
Uncle Alan Mightn't that be a sensible idea?

Music as they go towards Tom's bedroom, Uncle Alan pausing for a second to pick up the morning paper and post

Lights up on Tom's bedroom. He is still on the floor, head resting on the bed. There is no sign of Hatty, or the oil-lamp

Aunt Gwen and Uncle Alan enter

They look over the bed and see Tom

Aunt Gwen Thank heaven.

Uncle Alan End of problem. Told you.

Aunt Gwen Why's he on the floor? And the door was open...

Uncle Alan He must have gone sleepwalking.

Aunt Gwen Sleepwalking? Why?

Uncle Alan (*refraining from saying "what a stupid question"*) Well, it happens.

Aunt Gwen (*quietly putting Tom's slipper beside him and ushering Uncle Alan out*) We'd better not say anything. (*She knocks on the door*) Tom, time to get up! Breakfast!

Music as Tom wakes. He registers surprise at being on the floor, then remembers. He looks on the bed and is disappointed Hatty is not there

Meanwhile Aunt Gwen and Uncle Alan exit to get ready for breakfast

Tom puts on his slipper and his dressing-gown and leaves the bedroom

SCENE 6

The Lights fade up on breakfast

Tom joins Uncle Alan and Aunt Gwen; he is reading the paper, she is sorting the post

Aunt Gwen A letter for you, Tom. (*She hands it to him*)

Tom opens it, and starts to read

Lights up on Peter

Peter (*writing*) Dear Tom, beware!

Aunt Gwen opens a letter, and starts to read

Mum is writing to Aunt Gwen to say can you come home at the end of the week, because I miss you so much.

Aunt Gwen Well, Tom, it's home on Saturday, your mother says. Peter's really missing you.

Tom looks up, then returns to the letter

Peter (*writing*) Take no notice. I *do* miss you, but I love your letters, and want
  you to stay with Hatty so you can write more.
Uncle Alan (*looking up*) Well, be sorry to see you go, old chap.
Tom Can't I stay longer?
Aunt Gwen (*smiling*) Not unless we adopt you!

Uncle Alan laughs

Tom (*slowly*) If you *did* adopt me...
Aunt Gwen I was only joking, Tom.

Tom goes back to his letter

Peter (*writing*) What I'd really like is to join you and meet Hatty and all play
  together. Love, Peter.

The Lighting fades on Peter. Tom carefully folds up the letter

Tom (*thoughtfully*) What is Time?
Aunt Gwen Nearly half past nine. I really must get a move on. Shopping to
  do.
Tom No, Aunt Gwen, I mean, what is Time? How does Time work?

Aunt Gwen and Uncle Alan look at each other

Uncle Alan We ... er ... started to discuss Time the other day. You see, Tom,
  it all depends on which theory you believe...
Aunt Gwen (*quickly*) Well, if it's theories, I'll leave you both to it and get
  myself ready.

Aunt Gwen goes

Uncle Alan puts down his paper

Uncle Alan Time, Tom, is ... well, some people say it's relative. The time
  before Christmas may go very slowly, or appear to, whereas the time
  before an important exam flies by, or appears to. Or maybe the other way
  round! Another theory states...
Tom Time no longer. That's what the angel says.
Uncle Alan What's an angel got to do with it?
Tom That's just it. I don't know.
Uncle Alan Well, Tom, forget about angels. Think of a point in Time which
  we'll call A...
Tom (*more interested in his own thoughts*) I mean, how could Rip Van

Winkle have gone to sleep for one night ... well, he *thought* it was for one night ... and then woken up twenty years later?

Uncle Alan Rip Van Winkle's just a fairy tale. Now, Tom, point A...

Tom What about going *back* in time? Like time machines.

Uncle Alan Fantasy, Tom, pure fantasy! Come back to point A. I'll do you a diagram... (*He starts to draw on the back of an envelope*)

Tom (*working it out for himself*) But it's true! Hatty's present is my past. But every night Hatty's present is *my* present. And hours in Hatty's present are only minutes in *my* present. Like Rip Van Winkle in reverse.

Uncle Alan (*still drawing, not listening*) Uhuh.

Tom If I could only stay in Hatty's present for days, weeks, months even, I could come back to *my* present as though I'd never been away. Time no longer!

The clock chimes as the Lighting fades

SCENE 7

1950s traffic noises

Lighting reveals Mrs Bartholomew with the shopping, looking thoughtfully from a bridge

Aunt Gwen enters, in hat and coat, carrying a shopping bag

Aunt Gwen Mrs Bartholomew! I saw you standing on the bridge. I wondered if ... are you all right?

Mrs Bartholomew doesn't react, but stares ahead

Gwen Kitson, first floor back.

Mrs Bartholomew I love the river.

Aunt Gwen Shame it's so dirty, though. Alan says it's pollution. Dreadful stuff from the factories. It kills all the fish and coats all the healthy green weeds with that brown, furry stuff. It's not right.

Mrs Bartholomew (*smiling*) I see lush meadows, weeping willows, waterfowl.

Aunt Gwen Oh. I see houses, broken bottles and rusty tins.(*She clearly thinks Mrs Bartholomew is mad*) Well, bye then, Mrs Bartholomew.

Aunt Gwen goes

Mrs Bartholomew I see summer sunshine, boating, bathing...

The 1950s street noises change into the happy sounds of 1890s folk splashing in the water, oars creaking, laughter

I see winter frost glinting...

The Lighting changes. Snow falls

...I see one special winter. The great freeze. Every tree muffled in white. Ice gripping the flooded meadow, the river a frozen ribbon...

Sounds of skating, laughing, a hurdy-gurdy playing

...the skating-party!

The cast enter in 1890s winter coats and gloves. They perform a stylised skating mime in the snow. It is almost dreamlike, possibly in silhouette

The Lighting on Mrs Bartholomew fades and she exits as the music becomes louder

Tom enters and watches

Suddenly one of the skaters separates from the group and approaches. It is Hatty

Hatty Tom! You've come back!

They exchange their outstretched vertical palms greeting

Tom Of course.
Hatty I hoped you would. Aren't you cold?
Tom No.
Hatty But ... you're thinner.
Tom (*feeling his stomach*) I don't think so, Hatty.
Hatty No, I mean thinner *through*. I can't see you so clearly. But never mind, isn't this wonderful?

The skating continues behind them

Everyone's here. The Chapman girls, Young Barty—James's friend— and skating's such fun. Come on, try it...

Hatty skates, encouraging Tom to join her. He tries, in spite of wearing one slipper and one bare foot. He manages a slide

Tom (*enjoying it*) Whoooo! (*He tries another, but this time falls over and laughs. He stands up again*) If I only had skates!

Hatty (*joining him*) You need skates, Tom. Like mine.

Tom (*having an idea*) Hatty, where do you keep your skates?

Hatty In the boot cupboard in the hall.

Tom I've got an idea! Will you promise me something?

Hatty Depends what it is.

Tom Well, it may sound silly, but will you promise me from now on to keep your skates, always, when you're not using them, in that secret place you showed me in your bedroom cupboard, under the floorboards?

Hatty That *is* silly, Tom.

Tom Promise, Hatty. Please. Keep them there.

Hatty But ... oh, very well. I promise.

Tom Thank you. I must go. Bye, Hatty.

Tom goes

Hatty (*calling after him*) But, Tom. That means I should have to leave the skates behind altogether if I went away from here!

But Tom has gone. Hatty shakes her head

A voice interrupts her thoughts—Young Barty

Young Barty Miss Hatty! What are you doing all by yourself? We're about to have a race!

Hatty (*smiling*) Coming, Barty!

The Lighting fades as she turns back to join the other skaters

SCENE 8

Tom's bedroom. Dim lighting

Music as Tom silently enters, collecting his slipper en route

He carefully turns on the bedside light and angles the shade towards the cupboard, then opens the cupboard door. He delves beneath the floorboards. Almost unable to believe it, he brings out a brown paper package. There is a note slipped under the string. Tom sits on the bed to read it

Tom (*reading*) To whomever may find this. This package is left in this place...

Hatty's voice is heard joining Tom's

Hatty enters the frozen meadow area

Tom ⎫
Hatty ⎭ *(together)* …in fulfilment of a promise I once made to a little boy.

Hatty Signed. Harriet Melbourne…

Tom June the twentieth, eighteen *(peering)* something… (*Excitedly he unwraps the parcel and carefully, triumphantly, brings out and holds up the skates*) It worked, Peter, it worked! (*As he talks, he turns out the bedside light and leaves the bedroom, taking the skates back to the frozen meadow area*) Next day I rubbed the rust off Hatty's skates and oiled the leather of the boots and the straps. They were almost a perfect fit. And they were proof, Peter, positive proof! Time no longer! That night I met Hatty again…

Hatty joins Tom. They hold up their identical skates, then hang them somewhere visible each side of the stage

…and, impossible to believe but true, we skated together, wearing the same skates!

Exciting music as Hatty and Tom slowly begin to skate, miming on the spot, facing front

Hatty Oh, Tom, I feel as if I could skate to the end of the world, as if all the world were ice!

Tom *(laughing)* Come on, Hatty. Let's go! To the end of the world!

They speed up

Hatty I feel as I've never felt before. As free as a bird. I want to go so far. So far!

Tom You can, Hatty. You can!

They skate with joy and exhilaration. Hatty radiant

On and on we skated, Peter. Castleford left behind us. River banks flashing past. Under bridges. Past ice-locked ferryboats, on and on, mile upon mile … until…

Hatty Tom! Look! The tower of Ely Cathedral!

They slow down, looking up in awe. Mysterious music

Tom Peter, look at the postcard I sent you. The tower of Ely Cathedral. We're here!

Hatty Let's go inside! Let's climb the tower!

The Lights fade a little as they collect their skates and start to climb, going round and round. Meanwhile, the Lights fade up on Peter, in his pyjamas, looking at the postcard. Music

Shadowy figures enter and move around

Slowly, Peter, drawn by the postcard, joins them, wandering among them. They don't see him. Tom and Hatty reach the top of the tower and look out at the view. The shadowy figures become a group of sightseers, led by the tower-keeper. Peter is among them, in his pyjamas, carrying the postcard

Tower-keeper Over there, ladies and gentlemen, you can see the spires of Castleford, over here the city of Peterborough and in *that* direction lies King's Lynn and the sea.

Suddenly Peter sees Tom. During the following, Hatty regards the two boys in wonderment. Everyone else is turned away

Peter (*calling*) Tom!

Tom (*going to him*) Peter! You looked at the postcard!

Peter Yes. I couldn't sleep. I was thinking of you.

Peter ⎤ (*together*) Wow!
Tom ⎦

Peter But, Tom, where's the garden? That's what I really want to see. And Hatty.

Tom The garden's back there. And Hatty's here.

Peter Where?

Tom There! Looking at you! The one carrying skates.

Peter That's not Hatty!

Tom It is!

Peter That's a grown-up woman!

Tom looks at Hatty

Tower-keeper Time to go down again, if you please, ladies and gentlemen!

Peter She's grown-up!

The scene begins to clear as the visitors leave. Peter fades away, too, as if by magic

Tom and Hatty are left. The Lighting changes, to suggest they are back by the river. Tom is thoughtful

Hatty Who was he? *What* was he? He was unreal-looking, just like you.
Tom He was my brother, Peter. But he's real, Hatty. Real like me.
Hatty It's late. We'd better get back.

They start to put on their skates   As they cure

   Suddenly they hear Young Barty as he enters   down stairs.

Young Barty Miss Hatty? It *is* you. I was sure it was. (*He is eager, yet politely shy*)

Hatty reacts similarly to him

Tom Who's this?
Hatty (*ignoring Tom, greeting young Barty*) Barty! Good afternoon.
Young Barty (*raising his hat*) Good afternoon, Miss Hatty. Nearly good evening!
Hatty Yes. We were… (*She realizes that young Barty cannot see Tom*) That is to say, *I* was about to skate home.
Young Barty But it's nearly dark. Let me give you a lift.
Hatty Really?
Young Barty My horse and gig are at your service!
Hatty Thanks, Barty.

Music as actors create a gig from chairs. Young Barty leads Hatty to it and helps her aboard. Tom climbs aboard too. And Young Barty, who drives. Hatty is in the middle. The sound of the horse, clip-clopping on its way

Young Barty Did you skate all the way to Ely, Miss Hatty?
Hatty Yes. It was wonderful.
Young Barty That's quite an achievement. Few ladies would attempt to skate so far on their own. I'm full of admiration.

Hatty smiles

Tom She wasn't on her own.
Young Barty My mother and father once skated from Castleford to Ely and beyond, in their courting days. She remembers nearly falling asleep and half-dreaming she was skating far out to sea!
Hatty (*smiling*) I climbed the tower.

Tom So did I, Hatty. We climbed it together.
Hatty The view was breathtaking.
Young Barty You know I've never done that? Perhaps … would you like
to … maybe I could accompany you there … one day.
Hatty Yes, Barty. I'd really like that.

*She smiles as the gig clip-clops onward. Barty smiles, too, but Tom looks
excluded. The Lighting fades*

SET COMES BACK IN

SCENE 9

The clock chimes

*On chime nine, the Lights fade up in Tom's bedroom. Tom is in bed. He tosses
and turns. He is having a nightmare*

Shadowy figures are gathered below

The clock strikes thirteen

Voices—live and/or recorded—echo in Tom's head

Voice Thirteen.
Voice Take your chance.
Aunt Gwen Well, Tom, it's home tomorrow.
Voice Your last chance.
Voice Last chance.
Voice Go to Hatty.
Voice Stay with Hatty.
Voice Stay for ever.
Voices TIME NO LONGER!
Uncle Alan Fantasy, Tom, pure fantasy!

Distorted clock chimes punctuate the voices

Voice Take your chance.
Voice Last chance.

*Tom gets up and, as though sleepwalking, makes his way down towards the
door*

Peter She's a grown-up woman!

Hatty Yes, Barty, I'd really like that.
Voices TIME NO LONGER.

The shadowy figures surround Tom and bar his path

Abel Get you gone. Back to Hell where you came from!
Aunt Gwen Home tomorrow! Home tomorrow!
Mrs Bartholomew Who's been meddling with my clock?
Voices TIME NO LONGER.

Tom begins to panic, trying to escape

James She should meet more people. Make friends.
Hatty Yes, Barty, I'd really like that.
Uncle Alan Fantasy, Tom, pure fantasy!

Perhaps the voices overlap and increase in intensity. At last, Tom turns up towards the clock

    Suddenly a huge angel appears, bearing down on Tom

Lighning flashes. Thunder echoes. A human scream, just as we heard when the fir tree fell earlier

Voices TIME
          NO
          LONGER!

Tom turns and runs through the garden door. The angel disappears. Immediately we hear a high pitched sound and a bright light hits Tom. Tom screams

The echoing sound of dustbins clattering to the concrete backyard floor

Tom, unable to reach the garden, crumples as the shadowy figures withdraw

Tom (*calling wildly*) Hatty! Hatty! Where are you, Hatty? Hatty! Hatty!

An eerie silence

    Then Uncle Alan, in his dressing-gown, enters running

Uncle Alan (*scooping Tom up*) It's all right, old chap. Wake up. It's all right.

Aunt Gwen enters, in her dressing-gown

Uncle Alan hands Tom to her

Aunt Gwen helps Tom off

Uncle Alan closes the door, then turns to meet Mrs Bartholomew, who enters in her dressing-gown

Mrs Bartholomew Do you need me?
Uncle Alan No, no, Mrs Bartholomew. There's no problem.
Mrs Bartholomew What's happened? I heard a crash.
Uncle Alan It wasn't burglars. Only dustbins knocked over in the backyard. Please go back to bed.
Mrs Bartholomew But it's past midnight.
Uncle Alan Yes, I'm sorry. My nephew, Mrs Bartholomew. A case of sleepwalking. He's done it before.
Mrs Bartholomew I heard a cry.
Uncle Alan He hasn't hurt himself, I'm glad to say.
Mrs Bartholomew Someone was calling.
Uncle Alan Let me see you back to your door.
Mrs Bartholomew Someone was calling.
Uncle Alan I'm sorry you were disturbed. It won't happen again.

He leads her off

Mrs Bartholomew Someone was calling…

The Lighting fades as the clock strikes five

SCENE 10

Lights up on Tom, fully dressed, standing with his suitcase

Aunt Gwen enters

Aunt Gwen All set, Tom?

Tom nods

How are you feeling? Better?

Tom nods. Aunt Gwen kisses him

Uncle Alan's getting the car ready.

Tom I'm sorry, Aunt Gwen. About last night.

Aunt Gwen It wasn't your fault, Tom. Once you're home, back with Peter, you'll be fine. Won't you?

Tom nods, uncertain

Uncle Alan enters

Uncle Alan That wretched old woman. Why can't she leave well alone?

Aunt Gwen Mrs Bartholomew? What does she want now?

Uncle Alan An apology for the disturbance last night. Of course I gave her one at the time, and I apologised again just now—but she says the boy himself must go to her.

Aunt Gwen That's outrageous. I shouldn't dream of making Tom go. I shall tell her so.

Uncle Alan Careful, Gwen. She is our landlady…

Tom I'll go to her. I ought to. I don't mind.

Aunt Gwen and Uncle Alan look at each other as Tom leaves them

SCENE 11

The Lighting changes

Tom and Mrs Bartholomew meet

At first she seems forbidding. Tom doesn't look her in the eye

Mrs Bartholomew Yes?

Tom I've come to say sorry…

Mrs Bartholomew Don't be afraid. Let me see your face.

Tom looks up

Is your name Tom?

Tom How did you know that? Did Uncle Alan tell you?

Mrs Bartholomew (*shaking her head*) You're real. (*Touching his arm*) A real, flesh-and-blood boy. The Kitsons' nephew. And late last night…

Tom Yes. I'm sorry.

Mrs Bartholomew You called out. You woke me up.

Tom Yes. I'm really sorry.

Mrs Bartholomew You called a name…

Tom sees something. He moves DS

Tom (*as if in a dream*) That's the barometer from the Melbournes' hall. (*He looks at a photo*) And that's a photo of Young Barty.
Mrs Bartholomew Taken soon after we were married.
Tom You married Young Barty?
Mrs Bartholomew Yes, Tom. (*Gently*) I'm Hatty.

Tom, amazed and confused, looks at Mrs Bartholomew

I'm Hatty.
Tom You can't be. Hatty was a girl in Queen Victoria's reign. That began in 1837.
Mrs Bartholomew I wasn't born then. Victoria was an old lady when I was a girl. I'm a late Victorian.

Tom stares at Mrs Bartholomew. Slowly she holds out her hand. He does the same. They both upturn their palms in their accustomed special way. As their palms nearly touch, Tom is convinced

Tom (*thrilled*) You were Hatty! You *are* Hatty. You're really Hatty!
Mrs Bartholomew (*nodding*) Come and sit down, Tom.
Tom (*smiling*) Thank you... Hatty.
Mrs Bartholomew I haven't seen you since...
Tom ...Young Barty gave us a lift!
Mrs Bartholomew No, since the evening before Young Barty and I were married.
Tom I never saw you then.
Mrs Bartholomew But I saw you Tom, on the lawn. There was a terrifying storm. A high wind. Lightning...
Tom (*remembering*) The tall fir tree crashed to the ground.
Mrs Bartholomew Yes!
Tom And I heard a scream. From upstairs!
Mrs Bartholomew I was watching from the window. Frightened.
Tom It was you screaming!
Mrs Bartholomew Next day, Midsummer's Day, Barty and I were married. We went to live in the Fens.
Tom Were you happy?
Mrs Bartholomew Oh, yes, And things went well for us. Much better than for my cousins here.
Tom What happened?
Mrs Bartholomew As the years went by, the family business grew less successful. Hubert and Edgar went off and James carried on alone. But eventually he had to sell most of the land and finally the house. Barty and

I came over for the auction. It was sad to see they were building houses in the garden...

Tom ...our garden...

Mrs Bartholomew Yes, our garden. But Barty bought some furniture, the barometer...

Tom ...the grandfather clock...

Mrs Bartholomew ...of course, the clock—I'd always loved the angel—and best of all, he bought the house.

Tom And you moved in.

Mrs Bartholomew Not then. We were very happy in the Fens. We turned this house into flats.

Tom Did you and Barty have children?

Mrs Bartholomew (*warmly*) Oh, yes. Two fine sons. They were both killed in the Great War. And then, years later, Barty died...

Tom And you came back here!

Mrs Bartholomew I did.

Tom And since then, you've often gone back in time, haven't you?

Mrs Bartholomew Gone back in time?

Tom Gone back into the past.

Mrs Bartholomew When you're my age, Tom, you live in the past a great deal. You remember it, you dream of it. Recently I've dreamed a great deal of you and the garden and what it was like to feel lonely, to long for someone to play with.

Tom But that was what *I* wanted here, stuck indoors. Someone to play with. Somewhere to play.

Mrs Bartholomew Somehow we found each other, Tom.

Tom Mrs Bartholomew, I mean Hatty, these last few nights you've hardly dreamt of the garden at all. You've dreamt of winter and skating, haven't you?

Mrs Bartholomew Of skating to Ely, of growing up, of Barty.

Tom (*to himself*) And less of me.

Mrs Bartholomew And last night I dreamt of my wedding day and of leaving here.

Tom And last night, I found the garden wasn't there any more.

Mrs Bartholomew And you called out.

Tom And you heard me.

Mrs Bartholomew I couldn't believe you were real, until I saw you just now.

Tom We're both real. Then and now. It's as the angel said...

Tom ⎫
          ⎬ (*together*) Time no longer.
Mrs Bartholomew ⎭

Aunt Gwen (*off; calling*) Tom, dear, the car's ready!

Tom stands

Tom (*calling off*) Coming, Aunt Gwen. (*To Mrs Bartholomew*) I'm sorry,
  I go home today.
Mrs Bartholomew But you'll be back. You always come back, Tom.
Tom Yes.
Mrs Bartholomew And bring your brother, the one I saw at Ely.
Tom Peter. I will. (*Suddenly*) Hatty, what happened to Abel?
Mrs Bartholomew He married Susan of course!
Tom Good. He could see me too, you know. He knew our secret!
Mrs Bartholomew Our secret. (*She almost whispers*) Let's keep it our
  secret. For always?
Tom For always.

Uncle Alan enters, carrying Tom's suitcase, followed by Aunt Gwen

Uncle Alan Sorry, Mrs Bartholomew. Tom, we really must be off.

Music as Mrs Bartholomew stands

Tom (*formally*) Goodbye, Mrs Bartholomew. Thank you very much for
  seeing me.
Mrs Bartholomew (*formally*) I shall look forward to our meeting again.
  (*She holds out her hand*)

*They perform their usual outstretched vertical palm non-touching greeting.
Then suddenly—for the first time—their palms touch, and then their fingers
interlock in warm friendship. Then Tom turns and walks towards his uncle
and aunt. Suddenly he turns back and runs to Mrs Bartholomew. They hug
warmly. Uncle Alan and Aunt Gwen watch in amazement*

Then Tom kisses his surprised aunt and leaves, followed by Uncle Alan

The Lighting fades on Mrs Bartholomew

*Aunt Gwen waves offstage. (Perhaps we hear the car drive off.) She turns
back and suddenly notices something. She picks up an antique pair of skates.
She looks at them, wondering where on earth they could have come from. The
clock chimes for the last time*

The Lighting fades

CURTAIN

FURNITURE AND PROPERTY LIST

Further dressing may be added at the director's discretion

ACT I

Scene 1

On stage: Grandfather clock
Clock winding handle
Book
Tree
Bed
Chairs
Curtains on windows

Personal: **Mrs Bartholomew:** clock key

Scene 2

On stage: As before

Off stage: **Tom**'s suitcase (**Uncle Alan**)

Personal: **Uncle Alan:** wrist-watch (worn throughout)

Scene 3

On stage: As before

Personal: **Tom:** picture postcard, pen (carried throughout)
Peter: postcard

Scene 4

Set: **Tom**'s slippers

Off stage: Coal scuttle (**Susan**)

Personal: **Peter:** letter, pen (carried throughout)

Scene 5

Set: Newspaper

Scene 6

On stage: As before

Off stage: Bird (**SM**)
              Wheelbarrow, garden tools (**Abel**)
              Package containing sandwiches (**Susan**)
              Skipping rope (**Hatty**)

Personal: **Hatty:** note

Scene 7

On stage: As before

Personal: **Tom:** thermometer
              Aunt Gwen: wrist-watch (worn throughout)
              Uncle Alan: pipe

Scene 8

On stage: As before

Off stage: Apples (**The Cousins**)

Personal: **Edgar:** hazel-switch, apple

Scene 9

On stage: As before

Off stage: Goose-feathers (**Hatty**)

Scene 10

Set: Stave of yew
              Kitchen knife
              String
              Arrows

Off stage: Pans, garden implements (**The Cousins**)
                Doll (**Small Hatty**)

Scene 11

Set: Encyclopaedia

Scene 12

Set: Toy

Off stage: Wheelbarrow (**Abel**)
                Bible (**Abel**)

Scene 13

On stage: As before

ACT II

Scene 1

On stage: As before

Off stage: Tray (**Susan**)
                Office ledgers (**James**)

Scene 2

On stage: As before

Scene 3

On stage: **Hatty**'s tray
                Bundle containing book, toy, photograph

Off stage: Oil lamp (**Susan**)

Scene 4

On stage: As before

Scene 5

Set: Morning paper
Post

Off stage: **Tom**'s slipper (**Aunt Gwen**)
Shopping basket (**Mrs Bartholomew**)
Razor (**Uncle Alan**)

Personal: **Aunt Gwen:** curlers
Uncle Alan: shaving foam on face

Scene 6

Set: Newspaper
Letters
Pencil

Scene 7

On stage: As before

Off stage: Shopping bag (**Mrs Bartholome**)
Shopping bag (**Aunt Gwen**)

Scene 8

Set: Brown paper package with note, containing skates

Scene 9

On stage: As before

Scene 10

Set: Suitcase

Scene 11

Set: Photo

Off stage: **Tom**'s suitcase (**Uncle Alan**)

LIGHTING PLOT

Practical fittings required: oil lamp, bedside light
Various settings. The same throughout

ACT I, Scene 1

To open: Dim lighting

No cues

ACT I, Scene 2

To open: Snap lights up to bright normality

Cue 1   **Actors** freeze   (Page 2)
              Change lighting

ACT I, Scene 3

To open: Lights up on **Tom**'s bedroom

Cue 2   **Tom**: "This card is a picture…"   (Page 3)
              Lights up on **Peter**

Cue 3   **Tom** leaves   (Page 3)
              Fade lights on **Tom***; hold on* **Peter**

Cue 4   **Peter**: "Aunt Gwen bakes a great cake!"   (Page 3)
              Fade lights on **Peter**

ACT I, Scene 4

To open: Lights up on clock

Cue 5   **Tom** enters his room   (Page 4)
                 Bright up lights on **Tom**'*s room*

Cue 6   **Peter** appears   (Page 4)
                 Bright up lights on **Peter**

Cue 7   **Aunt Gwen** turns off the light   (Page 5)
                 Cut lighting on **Tom**

Cue 8   **Tom** turns on bedside light   (Page 5)
                 Backup lamp light

Cue 9   **Uncle Alan** turns off bedside light   (Page 5)
                 Cut bedside light backup

Cue 10   Clock starts to strike   (Page 5)
                 Fade lights on **Peter**; *bring up shaft of moonlight*
                     on **Tom** *in bed*

Cue 11   **Tom** very slowly opens door   (Page 7)
                 Moonlight floods in

Cue 12   **Tom** emerges "outside"   (Page 7)
                 Lighting effects as he speaks

Cue 13   **Tom** looks mystified   (Page 7)
                 Lights up on **Peter**

Cue 14   **Tom**: "It was real."   (Page 8)
                 Fade lights on **Tom**, *in bed*

Cue 15   **Peter**: "B.A.R... Tom."   (Page 8)
                 Fade lights on **Peter**

ACT I, SCENE 5

To open: Overall general lighting

Cue 16   **Mrs Bartholomew** starts to wind the clock   (Page 10)
                 Fade lighting down

ACT I, Scene 6

To open:	Bring up lighting on **Tom**'s bedroom	
Cue 17	**Tom** opens garden door *Light floods in*	(Page 10)
Cue 18	**Tom** explores garden *Brighten and colour scene with lighting effects*	(Page 10)
Cue 19	**Tom** heads back towards garden door *Fade lighting on* **Abel**	(Page 11)
Cue 20	**Tom** reaches garden door *Sudden flash of lightning, then more lightning*	(Page 11)
Cue 21	**Tom** heads for his room *Bring up lights on* **Peter**	(Page 11)
Cue 22	**Peter**: "Double wow!" *Fade lights on* **Peter**	(Page 12)

ACT I, Scene 7

To open:	Lighting on **Tom**'s room	
Cue 23	**Aunt Gwen** exits *Fade lights on* **Tom**'s *room, bring up lights on sitting-room*	(Page 12)
Cue 24	**Uncle Alan** and **Aunt Gwen** sit puzzled *Fade lights*	(Page 13)

ACT I, Scene 8

To open: Lighting on garden

No cues

ACT I, Scene 9

To open: As before

Cue 25   **Tom** and **Hatty** perform their greeting   (Page 21)
                Fade lights

ACT I, SCENE 10

To open: Lighting on **Peter**

Cue 26   **Peter**: "Now I'm teaching Hatty…"   (Page 21)
                Lights up on **Tom** *and* **Hatty**

Cue 27   **Hatty** fires arrow and looks at **Tom**   (Page 23)
                Fade lights on **Peter**

Cue 28   **Hatty** stumbles away   (Page 25)
                Change lighting

Cue 29   **Tom** closes the door and returns to his room   (Page 26)
                Fade lighting

ACT I, SCENE 11

To open: Lighting on **Tom**'s bedroom

Cue 30   **Tom**: "The plot thickens…"   (Page 27)
                Fade lighting

ACT I, SCENE 12

To open: Lighting on garden

Cue 31   **Tom**: "Can he?"   (Page 29)
                Fade lighting

ACT I, SCENE 13

To open: Lighting on **Peter**

Cue 32   **Peter**: "Then I could meet Hatty…"   (Page 30)
                Lights up on **Tom** *and* **Hatty**

| *Cue* 33 | **Peter**: "Love, Peter." | (Page 30) |
| | *Fade lights on* **Peter** | |

| *Cue* 34 | Nightmare music after **Hatty**'s fall | (Page 30) |
| | *Lighting effects* | |

| *Cue* 35 | **Voices**: "Time … no … longer!" | (Page 31) |
| | *Black-out* | |

ACT II, Scene 1

To open: Dim lighting

| *Cue* 36 | **Tom**: "… or even "alive but can't live long"?" | (Page 33) |
| | *Bring lights up on* **Peter** | |

| *Cue* 37 | **Aunt Grace** and **James** take their positions | (Page 34) |
| | *Fade lights a little; keep lighting same on* **Peter** | |

ACT II, Scene 2

To open: Lights up in **Aunt Grace**'s bedroom, fade on **Peter**

| *Cue* 38 | **Tom** exits | (Page 36) |
| | *Fade lights on* **Aunt Grace** *and pick up on* **Tom** | |

| *Cue* 39 | **Tom**: "…with that monster of an aunt!" | (Page 36) |
| | *Lights up on* **Peter** | |

| *Cue* 40 | **James** emerges, closing the door | (Page 36) |
| | *Fade lighting on* **Peter** | |

ACT II, Scene 3

To open: Lights up on **Hatty** in bed. General lighting fades during the scene

| *Cue* 41 | **Hatty**: "I'd never want to hear that." | (Page 37) |
| | *Lights are at dusk level* | |

| *Cue* 42 | **Susan** makes oil lamp shine brightly | (Page 37) |
| | *Backup oil lamp* | |

ACT II, SCENE 4

To open: Dim general lighting, backup oil lamp

Cue 43   **Hatty** turns down the oil-lamp   (Page 41)
            Reduce oil lamp backup

Cue 44   **Tom** goes to sleep by the bed   (Page 41)
            Fade lighting

ACT II, SCENE 5

To open: Lights up in hall

Cue 45   **Uncle Alan** and **Aunt Gwen** go towards **Tom**'s room   (Page 42)
            *Lights up on **Tom**'s bedroom*

ACT II, SCENE 6

To open: Lighting on breakfast

Cue 46   **Tom** starts to read letter   (Page 43)
            *Lights up on **Peter***

Cue 47   **Peter**: "Love, Peter."   (Page 44)
            *Fade lights on **Peter***

Cue 48   **Tom**: "Time no longer!"   (Page 45)
            Fade lighting

ACT II, SCENE 7

To open: Lighting on **Mrs Bartholomew** outdoors

Cue 49   **Mrs Bartholomew**: "I see winter frost glinting…"   (Page 46)
            Change lighting to winter; snow effect

Cue 50   **Cast** perform skating sequence   (Page 46)
            *Fade lighting on **Mrs Bartholomew***

Cue 51   **Hatty** turns back to join other skaters   (Page 47)
            Fade lighting

ACT II, Scene 8

To open:	Dim lighting on **Tom**'s bedroom	
Cue 52	**Tom** turns on bedside light	(Page 47)
	Backup bedside light	
Cue 53	**Tom** turns off bedside light	(Page 48)
	Cut bedside light	
Cue 54	**Hatty** and **Tom** start to climb	(Page 49)
	Fade lights a little on **Tom** *and* **Hatty**; *bring up lights on* **Peter**	
Cue 55	**Peter** exits	(Page 49)
	Fade out light on **Peter**; *change to riverside lighting*	
Cue 56	**Hatty** and **Barty** smile	(Page 51)
	Fade lighting	

ACT II, Scene 9

To open:	Darkness	
Cue 57	Clock chimes nine times	(Page 51)
	Fade up lighting on **Tom**'s *bedroom*	
Cue 58	Huge angel appears, bearing down on **Tom**	(Page 52)
	Lights on angel; lightning flashes	
Cue 59	**Tom** turns and runs through garden door	(Page 52)
	Cut lights on angel	
Cue 60	High pitched sound is heard	(Page 52)
	Snap on bright light on **Tom**	
Cue 61	**Mrs Bartholomew**: "Someone was calling…"	(Page 53)
	Fade lighting	

ACT II, Scene 10

To open:	Lights up on **Tom**
No cues	

ACT II, Scene 11

To open: Change lighting to **Mrs Bartholomew**'s

Cue 62   **Tom** leaves, followed by **Uncle Alan**   (Page 57)
                Fade lighting on **Mrs Bartholomew**

Cue 63   Clock chimes for the last time   (Page 57)
                Fade lighting

EFFECTS PLOT

ACT I

Cue 27   **Hubert** and **Edgar** throw apple back and forth   (Page 18)
            Pincher barks

Cue 28   **Tom** and **Hatty** perform their greeting   (Page 21)
            Clock chimes

Cue 29   **Hatty** fires arrow toward greenhouse   (Page 22)
            Shattering glass noise

Cue 30   **Tom**: "It's not a very big river."   (Page 23)
            Sound of geese swimming

Cue 31   **Hatty**: "…and at last it reaches the sea."   (Page 23)
            Distant sound of geese

Cue 32   **Hatty**: "Quick."   (Page 24)
            Increase sound of geese, following **Tom** *and* **Hatty**

Cue 33   **Tom**: "The geese are following us!"   (Page 24)
            Increase geese squawking, developing into chaos as
               geese arrive in garden

Cue 34   **Cast** chase geese   (Page 24)
            Geese sounds and Pincher barking

Cue 35   Geese are banished   (Page 24)
            Fade geese sounds

Cue 36   Mysterious music plays   (Page 25)
            Distorted clock chime

Cue 37   **Small Hatty** looks at clock   (Page 25)
            Clock chimes

Cue 38   **Tom**: "The plot thickens…"   (Page 27)
            Clock chimes

Cue 39   **Tom**: "Can he?"   (Page 29)
            One chime of clock

Cue 40   **Abel** slams door shut   (Page 31)
            Sound of door bolt echoing eerily

Cue 41   **Tom**: "Hatty!"   (Page 31)
          Clock strikes

ACT II

Cue 42   **Mrs Bartholomew** and shadowy figures exit   (Page 32)
          Gradually increase clock ticking volume; then cut
            abruptly

Cue 43   **Peter**: "The clock was there, of course…"   (Page 33)
          Sound of clock ticking

Cue 44   **Tom** starts to climb stairs   (Page 33)
          Door slam

Cue 45   **Peter**: "I started to go through one, when suddenly…"   (Page 34)
          Door slam

Cue 46   **Hatty** looks affectionately at photograph   (Page 38)
          Clock chimes six

Cue 47   **Tom** and **Hatty** reach clock   (Page 38)
          Bong dinner gong

Cue 48   **All** except **Tom** and **Hatty** exit   (Page 39)
          Door slam

Cue 49   To open Scene 5   (Page 41)
          Clock chimes five times

Cue 50   **Tom**: "Time no longer!"   (Page 45)
          Clock chimes

Cue 51   To open Scene 7   (Page 45)
          Bring up 1950s traffic noises

Cue 52   **Mrs Bartholomew**: "…sunshine, boating, bathing…"   (Page 45)
          Change 1950s street noises into happy sounds of 1890s
            folk splashing in water, oars creaking, laughter

Cue 53   **Mrs Bartholomew**: "…the river a frozen ribbon…"   (Page 46)
          Sounds of skating, laughing, hurdy-gurdy playing

Cue 54   **Barty** drives **Hatty** and **Tom**   (Page 50)
            Sound of horse clip-clopping

Cue 55   To open Scene 9   (Page 51)
            Clock chimes

Cue 56   **Uncle Alan**: "Fantasy, Tom, pure fantasy!"   (Page 51)
            Distorted clock chimes

Cue 57   Lightning flashes   (Page 52)
            *Thunder echoing; human scream, same as when
              fir tree fell*

Cue 58   Angel disappears   (Page 52)
            High pitched sound

Cue 59   **Tom** screams   (Page 52)
            *Echoing sound of dustbins clattering on concrete
              back yard floor*

Cue 60   **Tom**: "Hatty! Hatty! Hatty!"   (Page 52)
            Cut noise to eerie silence

Cue 61   **Mrs Bartholomew**: "Someone was calling…"   (Page 53)
            Clock strikes five

Cue 62   **Aunt Gwen** regards pair of skates   (Page 57)
            Clock chime one last time

MADE AND PRINTED IN GREAT BRITAIN BY
LATIMER TREND & COMPANY LTD PLYMOUTH
MADE IN ENGLAND